Racial Opportunity Cost

Series edited by H. Richard Milner IV

OTHER BOOKS IN THIS SERIES

Urban Preparation
Chezare A. Warren

Justice on Both Sides
Maisha T. Winn

Truth Without Tears
Carolyn R. Hodges and Olga Welch

Millennial Teachers of Color
Edited by Mary E. Dilworth

Culturally Responsive School Leadership
Muhammad Khalifa

Science in the City
Bryan A. Brown

Race, Sports, and Education
John N. Singer

Start Where You Are, But Don't Stay There, Second Edition
H. Richard Milner IV

The Chicana/o/x Dream
Gilberto Q. Conchas and Nancy Acevedo

Restorative Justice in Education
Maisha T. Winn and Lawrence T. Winn

Teachers of Color Resisting Racism and Reclaiming Education
Rita Kohli

Stuck Improving
Decoteau J. Irby

Jim Crow's Pink Slip
Leslie T. Fenwick

Not Paved for Us
Camika Royal

Equality or Equity
Jeffrey M. R. Duncan-Andrade

Racial Opportunity Cost

The Toll of Academic Success on Black and Latinx Students

Terah Venzant Chambers

Harvard Education Press
Cambridge, Massachusetts

Library of Congress Cataloging-in-Publication Data is on file.
Paperback ISBN 978-1-68253-744-2

Published by Harvard Education Press,
an imprint of the Harvard Education Publishing Group

Harvard Education Press
8 Story Street
Cambridge, MA 02138

Cover Design: Ciano Design.
The typefaces in this book are Minion Pro, 11/14

Dedication

For the ancestors, whose unrelenting belief in the power of education fostered the educational opportunities from which I benefitted. My wildest dream is for this book to magnify the legacy and abundance of Black excellence. For my son, Langston Malcolm Toure Chambers, and all of those who come next: may you continue to know and be shielded by the brilliance of those who came before.

Contents

Series Foreword

IN HER NEW BOOK, *Racial Opportunity Cost: The Toll of Academic Success on Black and Latinx Students*, Terah Venzant Chambers challenges those of us committed to educational equity for minoritized young people to understand more deeply what it means to be Black *and* high achieving. She has produced an extraordinarily important book of stories and experiences of academically successful students of color that needs to be shared if we are to journey toward a more humane and liberating educational context. Black people achieve at high levels across nearly all fields and endeavors. They are CEOs at Fortune 500 companies; they are inventors and entrepreneurs; they succeed in athletics. And they are philanthropic—they give back to the communities in which they live and serve.

Just as Black people achieve at high levels in broader society, they also succeed in school. But what is essential to remember is that the scores of Black people who achieve across industry, metric, space, and place do so within and through systems that are deeply racist, sexist, xenophobic, homophobic, and classist. The field of education has produced scores of books that detail the success of young people, many times as "feel good" stories about overcoming adversity and challenging situations. However, what costs do these young people have to bear to learn and live, especially in places that attempt to strip them of their identity and, consequently, their humanity in the name of achievement? Venzant Chambers's book considers this and many other critically important questions: How do high-achieving students of color fare in educational systems not designed for them? How do they negotiate schooling structures that undermine their very essence? Drawing on astute and powerful interviews of Black and Latinx student at two highly selective universities, Venzant Chambers articulates and advances a framework for *racial opportunity cost* that captures the toll on student social and psychological well-being in exchange for academic success.

My own research shows that student outcomes are intimately connected to opportunity structures in a community, school, district, and classroom level; and they must be understood intersectionally in order to address what have traditionally been called achievement gaps. My work also demonstrates that gaps in achievement—too often synonymously associated with test scores—are a direct result of opportunity gaps. The ROC framework advances our understanding of opportunity structures and how they should be viewed. In short and in sum, high-achieving students of color pay a price for the ways in which they are too often forced to "assimilate" into oppressive situations. The compelling student portraits offered in this book detail how they have to negotiate their racialized "actions, dress, and behavior" based on a set of expectations that follow white logics.

Venzant Chambers provides an important analytic tool to explain the data she has collected. Features of the racial opportunity cost framework include the need to examine the climate (or culture) of students' experiences, structure (places) of young people's experience, and the relationships involved in learning and development. I am thrilled to welcome this book into the Race and Education Series family. The stories captured in this book will leave readers yearning for the next word, the next chapter, the next insight. The themes of the stories are old and new, exciting and hurtful, disheartening and hopeful, challenging and inspirational.

Although not a prescription, Venzant Chambers sheds light on school-level mechanisms that can help educators build practices to address racial tensions that high-achieving Black and Latinx students experience. One of the remarkable contributions of the book is the explicit attention Venzant Chambers pays to student experiences that are implicit or completely hidden from well-intentioned educators. From my view, the book will serve as a wake-up call to educators who understand their primary roles to teach content only and not attend to other aspects of students' experiences, well-being, identity, and overall success. In other words, the book brings to light the datapoints and insights educators must consider beyond a test score to inaccurately capture high-achieving students' wholistic experience. The book concludes with recommendations and strategies for educators interested in decreasing racial opportunity costs in schools and for students.

Racial Opportunity Cost guides readers into interrogating and centering space—the location in which educators work. While many books focus on youth in urban and rural environments, this one provides implications for students in suburban and independent schools. Indeed, Black people experience challenges even as they succeed and achieve in mostly white contexts. I salute Venzant Chambers for work that adds to the resolve to dismantle structural and systemic racism in all forms.

H. Richard Milner IV
Cornelius Vanderbilt Distinguished Professor of Education
Department of Teaching and Learning
Vanderbilt University

REFERENCES

H. Richard Milner, *Start Where You Are But Don't Stay There: Understanding Diversity, Opportunity Gaps, and Teaching in Today's Classrooms*, 2nd ed. (Cambridge, MA: Harvard Education Press, 2020).

Preface

AS I WAS WORKING on this book and contemplating the best way to help readers understand the importance of focusing on the costs of academic success for Black and Latinx students, the world literally erupted in protest against the unjust murder by police of a Black man, George Floyd, in Minneapolis, Minnesota. I found myself writing in the middle of the dual pandemics of COVID-19 and anti-Black racial violence. While these protests captured the attention of people across the globe, it was an incident related to these events, not even 20 minutes from me, that truly highlighted the "why" of this book.

In June 2020, hundreds of community members in a community a few towns over from me came together at a virtual school board meeting to condemn racist and victim-blaming comments made by the then-superintendent about George Floyd, who had been killed by police just a few days before. In response to another district employee's post, the superintendent remarked, in part,

> It all starts with being a law abiding [*sic*] citizen—had [George Floyd] not paid with counterfeit money, had he not resisted, had he not been under the influence—then there would be no contact with officers; that does not excuse the officer; it just eliminates the conflict to begin with!! It starts with being a good citizen!

At the school board meeting, current students and graduates from racially minoritized backgrounds and their families shared story after story of how they were unfairly targeted and dehumanized, not just by the superintendent but by other teachers and school leaders. It became clear that the superintendent's comments were not isolated but represented a longstanding culture of institutional racism in the district. The costs of academic success for Black and Latinx students in white-normed schools were on full display in my own community and encapsulated the impetus for this book and so much of what I wanted it to convey. While I will outline more of the foundation and context for racial opportunity cost in the introduction to this book, I start with the story of what happened at the school board meeting for three reasons.

A PERSONAL CONNECTION

First, the stories shared by families at the school board meeting resonated with me on a personal level. I was writing a book amid these momentous times about the challenges Black and Latinx students face that was fueled by my own experiences in school. I grew up in Minnesota, but the demographics of the school I attended were much more similar to this nearby suburban community that had protested the superintendent's comments than Minneapolis. I had not grown up in the city where a constant police presence heightened the likelihood that my siblings or I could end up with a knee on our neck, as could have happened to my dad, who attended high school in Racine, Wisconsin. My parents moved to suburban Minnesota, where they hoped the "good" schools and "safe" community would protect their children from the anti-Black violence that fueled George Floyd's murder. Instead, it set us up for a different, more figurative inability to breathe. Listening to these families at the school board meeting share their stories about the mistreatment they experienced, I knew we shared the certain knowledge that our pain was just as genuine as what my parents feared we might experience in the city. It was just that no one talked about it and so too many suffered in silence, thinking they were the only one experiencing the profound isolation and targeted attacks. This book represents an opportunity to change that by putting a spotlight on these stories, highlighting just how common these experiences are for students from racially minoritized backgrounds in white-normed school settings.

I grew up in a pretty typical first ring suburban community in Minnesota. From the outside, the schools I attended were fairly racially diverse. The problem was that regardless of how racially diverse the school may have been, I was almost always the only Black student in my advanced placement and honors courses. And, because most of my schedule consisted of advanced classes, even my non-advanced classes, like gym, tended to include the same (mostly white) students from my other advanced classes. At the time, of course, I did not understand master schedules and the ways these stratifications can happen quite easily. Being the "only one" had a profound affect not only on me, but also on my white classmates. We never had teachers from racially minoritized backgrounds. The idea that Black and Latinx students did not take advanced classes was normalized to us—I felt like *I* was the outlier, the exception in my classes, not my Black peers in general and alternative education courses. I know that many of my white classmates saw it that way, too. When we applied to college and I got into my dream school, a friend commented that I had only gotten in because of affirmative action. On some subconscious level, I believed her, and I carried that feeling with me to the opening convocation of my first year of college. I was sitting in another room full of white students. In that moment, I was struck with the absolute certainty that a mistake had been made in the admissions office. Every day, I wrestled with feelings of stress and anxiety that continued to plague me throughout the year. On top of trying to deal with those feelings, I was ashamed for feeling that way and so I did not talk to anyone about it. After the school year ended, I withdrew from school, having earned a B average and the makings of an ulcer.

I think for many racially minoritized students with similar backgrounds, the story ends there. I know many Black and Latinx students who were absolutely capable of doing well in advanced courses and succeeding in college but did not—ending up either leaving college early, like me, or not enrolling in the high school courses that would prepare them for success in college. I know now that this is a common narrative. Luckily for me, my story did not end there. I ended up transferring to my local state university. There, I participated in a research program during the summer of my junior year that focused on providing opportunities for racially minoritized students to conduct research. My mentor, Dr. Martha Zurita, put me through her own rigorous research boot camp and rebuilt my confidence about my academic skills. She pushed me hard but also provided kind encouragement. She was my first example of the *warm demander* that I learned about from Vanessa Siddle Walker's work, adding color and texture to the sketched outline of the teacher I envisioned myself becoming.[1] She saw right through my façade of not wanting to go to graduate school. She saw my resistance for the fear and doubt it was masking. She showed me that the challenges I had encountered in school reflected larger institutional problems, teaching me that I could devote my time in graduate school to better understanding those problems and then conduct research to address them.

My time in graduate school at the University of Illinois provided exactly that education and so much more. Led by Dr. James Anderson, a preeminent historian of Black education, the program at that time was probably 80 percent Black and Latinx students and faculty. I had never even dreamed something like that was possible. I soaked up every conversation I heard, every nugget of wisdom shared about the history of Black education and all of the ways in which the legacy of institutionalized racism is present in our schools today. The anxiety I had felt for so many years about not feeling good enough or smart enough evaporated and was replaced with a simmering anger. I was angry that I had never been exposed to this information, that I had never had a teacher who looked like me, and that I had been left to feel responsible when the system let me down. I was also furious on behalf of the many Black and Latinx classmates I had had who would never have this experience—many had been failed by the system before they even had an inkling of what was happening to them. The anger fueled my commitment to become a professor to teach a new generation of educators and to also *be* that Black teacher I wish I had had.

Listening to the nearly seven hours of community stories at the virtual board meeting that summer catapulted me back to my own educational journey and offered an opportunity to reflect. It also reminded me that so many Black and Latinx students and families remain unaware that the pain they experienced in school is something they share with so many others. Thus, an important reason for this book is to help individuals from racially minoritized backgrounds understand—in a way that I wish I had known much earlier in my own life—that the hurt and trauma they carry with them is not unique and to put a name to it: racial opportunity cost.

LISTENING TO SILENCED STORIES

The pain that I shared with those community members brought up a second reason I felt it was important to start the book with this story: these stories deserve to be told. We deserve to understand the ways in which schools can damage racially minoritized students. I may have been reluctant to make the comparison between the murder of George Floyd and my own experiences in school had I not listened to the hours of testimony offered by these families and felt the pain in their stories. Part of my reluctance stems from my being a student of history, of knowing the explicit and brutal violence my ancestors endured in slavery and that my dad experienced growing up on a sharecropping farm in Mississippi before moving to Wisconsin—an experience about which he would never speak.

However, it is also precisely *because* I am a student of history that I understand that the same anti-Black racism that fueled slavery and the continuing violence against Black people also drives our mistreatment in schools. We are taught that racism is "a southern thing" in which the North did not participate. When we learn about this period of history at all, at best we are taught that people in the North were neutral observers in the atrocities. But as written about by journalists like Isabel Wilkerson and as depicted on shows like HBO's adapted series *Lovecraft Country*, Black people in the North did not escape racism.[2] Further, while the racism rampant in northern schools may not always have been as explicit, it was still just as pernicious. In every way that matters, Black and Latinx people have been systematically excluded from the educational opportunities in this country that were purportedly intended for everyone. Throughout the Jim Crow period of "separate but equal" that mandated racially segregated schools, Black children attended schools that did not receive the same resources afforded to white schools. However, through the powerful work of Black scholars like Vanessa Siddle Walker and James Anderson, we have learned that while these schools may not have been given the material resources to which they were entitled, they were filled with love and stood as models of academic excellence.[3]

Further, once the courts had finally ruled that *de jure* racial segregation in schools was unconstitutional (or, when in other areas where *de facto* segregation was more common, financial circumstances necessitated the inclusion of racially minoritized students), attending the same schools with white students did not lead to equal education. Instead, Black students were tracked into lower-level classes, were labeled with racist and ableist slurs, received inappropriate disciplinary consequences, and were generally subjected to what Bettina Love calls *spirit murder*.[4] What toll do those experiences take on a child? What is the impact of trying to survive in a system that has only ever held you in what W. E. B. Du Bois characterized as "amused contempt and pity"?[5] Though they did not use the term *racial opportunity cost*, the students and families who spoke at the school board meeting were naming it, outlining the acute and long-lasting impact that their time in the district had wrought. We must be ready to listen.

RECOGNIZING OUR RESPONSIBILITY

Finally, I start with this story of the community outpouring of grief and pain over their treatment in a predominantly white district because, as a professor in an educational leadership program who works with educators every day, I see it as our responsibility in leadership preparation programs to do things differently. I have now been teaching some version of a Leadership for Social Justice course for nearly 20 years. I have taught undergraduate students, some who aspired to become teachers, most who did not. I have taught at elite private colleges and large public universities. However, I have mainly taught at the graduate level, to students who themselves have often been working as school leaders for decades. In that time, I have found that the students who often have the least robust understanding not just of issues of race, but of the historical and institutional frameworks that influence our contemporary educational system, are the ones in leadership positions in our schools and districts. I do not say this to be critical of those leaders. In fact, if anything, it is an indictment of the training most receive in their teacher and leadership preparation programs. We have not come close to adequately helping our students understand the foundation from which many of these contemporary issues originate. If the people who are leading the district or the school are unaware of these issues, how can they be expected to ensure that the students in their care learn about them or, more importantly, to lead their schools and districts to understand, identify, and *change* the mechanisms to move toward more just school environments?

I want to be clear that I am not singling out this local community to make any sort of point about that district in particular. Rather, I share this story because that district is more the norm than we realize, the pain these community members shared more common than we know. One only needs to do an Internet search with keywords "racist comments about George Floyd" with "teacher," "principal," or "superintendent" to see that hundreds of similar incidents occurred in the wake of the tragedy. Grand Ledge stands out because in addition to happening in my local area, school leaders there afforded an opportunity for these racially minoritized community members' stories to be heard.

It is also true that the superintendent in question received a doctorate from Michigan State University in the same educational leadership program in which I teach, but before I was on the faculty. Indeed, many of the district's teachers and administrators have earned degrees from our College of Education. Given that context, what then is our responsibility for the harm that was perpetuated by the superintendent's comments? How should we have better educated these future educators about the legacy of race and racism in our schools? Of course, it is imperative that we better understand racially minoritized students' experiences in these spaces. We also have a responsibility to help educators understand their role in cultivating environments that affirm racially minoritized students.

I have to believe that it is possible to cultivate school spaces that are more supportive of and humanizing to racially minoritized students not only because it is at the core of the research that I do, but because I am now a mother of a Black son who is attending school in a predominantly white district, very much like the one that I attended in Minnesota. I have to believe—as a scholar, teacher, and mom—that he can emerge from this experience not just having survived, but thrived. I have to believe that achieving success will not have to be as costly for him and his classmates as it was for me and so many other Black and Latinx students.

Introduction

THIS BOOK is the culmination of over a decade of research examining what it costs Black and Latinx students to pursue academic success, work that I have done to help shed light on the hidden trauma these students have faced navigating the racialized norms and values that permeate their school spaces. In that time, I have written about the costs of academic success for high-achieving Black and Latinx students—what I now call *racial opportunity cost,* or ROC—and laid out the empirical and theoretical support for this work across a series of articles.[1]

But where did the idea for ROC originate? Earlier in my career, I was conducting research with Black students about their experiences in tracked math and English classes.[2] However, while my findings answered many questions, it raised others. In particular, the high-track students talked about feeling disconnected from other Black students in part because they did not have any meaningful interaction with them. I myself had witnessed these awkward interactions during our focus groups that brought Black students together to talk about their classroom experiences. Despite having been in the same schools together often for years, they barely knew each other. More and more often, the conversations with the high-track students in the study drifted away from tracking specifically and turned to the challenges they faced navigating their mostly white classrooms. That is, high-track students focused on the costliness of their academic paths.

At about the same time, I found myself preparing a lecture on racial disparities in education and read an article that made a passing reference to the economic concept of opportunity cost. In economics, opportunity cost refers to forgone choices or trade-offs—the adage that you can't have your cake and eat it, too. To offer an example, a teacher might use their prep hour to return an urgent phone call to a parent about their child.

While returning the call might be their best choice, it is not the only one. Making that call means taking time away from returning emails, catching up on grading, telling their fellow subject-area teachers about an idea for an upcoming lesson, or many other tasks—all of which are important. However, they use their time in the way they think best, and the task they could have done instead represents their opportunity cost.

Sitting in my office and preparing for my lecture that day, the passing reference to opportunity cost spoke to me in a different way. Something about the idea of making a choice and achieving a goal, but at the cost of something else, seemed to appropriately describe the patterns I had seen in my research on school tracking. It was when I turned to existing research to see how others had made sense of this phenomenon that I learned that our existing body of research focused primarily on the achievement aspect of the issue: on the one hand, offering explanations for the "underperformance" of students with lower test scores or grades, or recommendations of interventions that might help them improve. On the other hand, the smaller amount of research that addressed the experiences of students who had achieved more traditional markers of academic success focused more on what we could learn from them to support students who had not been as successful. While this research was important and compelling, I could find very little that concretely articulated the toll taken on the students as a result of these experiences, that challenged the premise that these students were not, in fact, okay. We were missing research that took up the idea that the experience of navigating the racialized norms governing academic achievement in their schools might be traumatizing even for those racially minoritized students who had seemingly succeeded at it.

Reading in my office about opportunity cost that day, I was struck with the idea of *racial* opportunity cost and its potential use as a construct to articulate this very issue. From there, I began compiling an extensive review of literature from relevant fields that provided the conceptual support for racial opportunity cost and designed a study that would allow me to explore it as a way to describe the experiences of Black and Latinx students navigating dominant normed spaces. However, this extant body of writing was directed toward a primarily researcher audience and was spread out across a number of separate articles. My hope was to write collectively one day about this research in a book for the practitioners whom I hoped would use this work to understand the factors in their classrooms, schools, and districts that increase students' racial opportunity cost—and take action to address them.

THEORY OF RACIAL OPPORTUNITY COST

Racial opportunity cost emerged from four interrelated propositions: two primary ideas relating to the role of the school environment and its impact on Black and Latinx students, and two supporting ideas that further clarify these primary propositions. All four propositions are grounded in established and widely accepted scholarship. Through the ROC framework, I connect and concretize ideas from these bodies of literature and establish relationships among them. The relationship between these propositions is represented in figure 1.

Proposition One: Schools create and perpetuate rules that govern expectations for academic success that are based on white racial logics

The fundamental idea that schools create and perpetuate rules for academic success that extend from white normative expectations has been widely established across an interdisciplinary array of research and is historically longstanding. For example, famed sociologist W. E. B. Du Bois wrote over a century ago of the toll taken on Black people from negotiating what he called "double-consciousness," in a world where "one ever feels his twoness, —an American, a Negro; two souls, two thoughts, two unreconciled strivings; two warring ideals in one dark body, whose dogged strength alone keeps it from being torn asunder."[3] At its core, racial opportunity cost attempts to flesh out the impact of these unreconciled strivings, to document that while not completely torn asunder, the Black and Latinx students who must take up this battle are nonetheless left with scars that deserve attention. And, perhaps most importantly, a fundamental premise of ROC is that we can and must foster school spaces that leave fewer wounds on Black and Latinx students.

The tension discussed by Black scholars like Du Bois has been echoed by prominent Latinx scholars. In her seminal book *Subtractive Schooling,* Angela Valenzuela discussed the ways in which expectations built on white middle-class expectations unfairly and often inaccurately reflect Mexican American culture.[4] For example, Valenzuela wrote about the importance of *educación* in many Mexican American families. Very different from its English cognate, *educación* includes valued ideas about what it means to be a good person, emphasizing ideas of respect and responsibility that are seen as important for everyone regardless of background—or what is known in these families as being *bien educado*. However, because norms for success in schools are narrowly tailored to white cultural values, Mexican American students' cultural values can be devalued. Even worse, schools with these restrictive white-normed expectations can require students to turn away from their cultural and language traditions if they want to be seen as successful, stripping them of important connections to their community.

Some readers may be feeling that following rules is an important marker for success for all students, not just Black and Latinx students. While there are some whispers of truth to this position, it does not tell the whole story and for that reason can be dangerous. Historians have documented the role schools have played in the socialization process, particularly in the twentieth century.[5] As the country began to urbanize as a result of the larger industrialization process, schools became an important mechanism to teach immigrants to the United States, those moving from rural communities, or even those from families experiencing poverty the "right way" to be American.[6] Teachers incorporated Americanization lessons into the curriculum, including some that had nothing to do with academics.[7] Importantly, however, these schools did not provide the *same* education to all students based on its role in reproducing existing social and class hierarchies.[8] Students from more affluent families received an education that supported their assumed matriculation to college and positions as managers and leaders by fostering exposure to the liberal arts and critical thinking. This left students in less-privileged positions with teachers and courses that reiterated the importance of being on time and following directions, skills that would foster their likely roles in factories and other worker positions.[9] The legacy of this system is still with us today, with schools continuing to teach what is known as the "hidden curriculum," those unwritten and unofficial messages about what behaviors are acceptable or how students should interact with others or view various social groups.[10] Importantly, we often do not even acknowledge these hidden practices despite their widespread use, which makes them more difficult to challenge. Indeed, the hidden curriculum in schools may even contradict the formal curriculum. For example, aspects of the formal or espoused curriculum may express a belief that all students can be successful or that academic opportunities will be made available to all students. However, in accordance with the hidden curriculum, actual practices in the school may actually reinforce inequities.

And yet, while it is true that schools have historically played an important socialization role for all students, there remains a separate and particular way in which racially minoritized students have been impacted by imbedded whiteness in our educational institutions and practices. Founding critical race theorists founders—including Derrick Bell, Kimberlé Crenshaw, Richard Delgado, Alan Freeman, Lani Guinier, Angela Harris, Cheryl Harris, Charles Lawrence, Mari Matsuda, Jean Stefancic, Patricia Williams, and others—broke from the critical legal theory tradition with which they were allied in recognition of the specific and pernicious racial logics they argued permeated the very foundation of legal theory. They lamented critical theorists' lack of focus on the operation of race and racism in society and worked to create a set of theoretical principles that better articulated their operation.[11]

Over time, scholars in other interdisciplinary fields, but particularly sociology, have contributed to our understanding of the ways in which notions of power—and specifically notions of power that are grounded in white supremacy—have shifted over time but never disappeared. Feagin has talked about this as the "white racial frame."[12] Moore's work examined the "white space" or "white institutional space" created in an elite law school.[13] Bonilla-Silva's writing helps us understand the ways a move away from overt, mainstream white supremacy has given way to a more pernicious form of color-blind racism.[14] In his later work, he referred to this underlying racialized structure as being guided by "White logics." Specifically, Zuberi and Bonilla-Silva referred to white logics as:

> A context in which White supremacy has defined the techniques and processes of reasoning about social facts. White logic assumes a historical posture that grants eternal objectivity to the views of elite Whites and condemns the views of non-Whites to perpetual subjectivity; it is the anchor of the Western imagination, which grants centrality to the knowledge, history, science, and culture of elite White men and classified "others" as people without knowledge, history, or science, as people with folklore but not culture.[15]

In accordance with white logics, white culture is always seen as correct and this perspective permeates all aspects of society. By definition then, non-white cultures are "incorrect" unless people from them very closely mirror these white norms and values. Particularly resonant about this particular description of the historical and institutional role of whiteness is how the term *logic* conveys the way in which this perspective is forced on others.

Unsurprisingly, schools play a central role in maintaining these white logics because not only are these spaces imbued with them, but schools are also the place where children *learn* them. Even the most seemingly neutral processes become infused with these norms. Another way to say this is that these school processes become *racialized*. Barajas and Ronnkvist theorized this idea of schools as racialized spaces, arguing that schools as organizational structures take on symbolic racial meanings that are based on white middle-class understandings.[16] Thus, even seemingly race-neutral practices have these white logics baked into them. As a result, even mundane aspects of the school day can have differential consequences for students. In this way, these logics transcend geographic or demographic definitions; they are present regardless of whether a space is urban or rural, resource-rich or resource poor, predominantly white or all Black—in all of these spaces, these white logics dictate the rules for the environment within which students, teachers, and other school personnel operate.

While some scholars have helped foster our understanding of the basic operation of schools as racialized spaces, others have focused on the consequences of them for students. For example, Lisa Delpit offered the term the "culture of power" and proposed five related aspects of power that are related to its operation.[17] Over thirty years ago, she provided language to help understand how dominant cultural narratives drove expectations in schools, particularly in language instruction, but certainly also more generally. Given that many of these racial codes are part of the hidden curriculum, Delpit's explicit framing provides an important step for educators to explicitly talk about, understand, and challenge them.

The research I have mentioned so far is helpful in understanding where these logics originate and the ways in which they impact our learning environments. However, one of the clearest examples that I encountered of how students *learn* and *internalize* these white logics came from Beth Hatt's work on the social construction of "smartness" in the earliest days of a student's educational journey.[18] In her year-long ethnography of a racially diverse kindergarten classroom, students and their teachers provided a powerful testimony of the pervasive nature of whiteness and its role in performative expectations related to academic achievement. Hatt said she chose kindergarten as her focus because it is the place where these societal values are first, and most explicitly, introduced into the educational system. In the kindergarten classroom she studied, "smartness" was not about what students knew. Rather, being "smart" was aligned with compliance with school and classroom behavioral expectations, which she also noted were rooted in racialized norms and values. Black students experienced increased surveillance, their actions closely and critically monitored. At the same time, Hatt noted repeatedly the ways in which white students, despite engaging in similar or sometimes worse behavior infractions, experienced more freedom simply because the teachers were not watching them as closely or with the same level of scrutiny as they were the Black students. The students learned that being "smart" meant conducting their behavior and speaking in particular ways. Devastatingly, both Black and white students in the classroom that year learned from the teachers that Black students were less smart because of these racialized expectations and the ways in which Black students were seen not to align with them. Repeatedly, Hatt noted that these indications were grounded in a complicated web of subjective classroom and school expectations in which students had become wholly entrapped by the end of the year.

These lessons, continually reinforced throughout a student's K–12 journey, provide a foundation for a lifetime of navigation and negotiation for students, with particularly negative consequences for racially minoritized students. The process Hatt identified in which students in kindergarten learn that these subjective rules connect with success only become more engrained and enmeshed in the daily schooling experience as students matriculate to higher grades. Increasingly, one's actual ability is less relevant than whether that aptitude meets with expectations[19]—that is, whether it is performed "correctly." Connecting Hatt's work with the previous assertion about white institutional space and schools as racialized spaces, the point is not whether the teachers in the classroom Hatt studied may have been racist or held racist beliefs about racially minoritized students. Rather, far more important to this conversation is that, individual beliefs notwithstanding, they were also acting as agents of broader institutional processes as reproducers of whiteness and expectations for school success that are grounded in them.

While it is important to focus on actions that can be taken at the school level, a point to recognize and reiterate is the significance of these deeper systemic processes. Teachers likely carried these racialized expectations to the classroom from their teacher-preparation programs, where they likely learned the "classroom management" strategies they used with students. These racialized expectations influence who becomes a teacher in the first place, with candidates from racially minoritized backgrounds weeded out by processes similar to those I shared from my personal experience as a high school student. Thus, my intention is not to blame educators, as we are all caught up in this larger system. Indeed, if any part of the system could be counted on to break this cycle, I put my faith in teachers as the people and schools as the place to do it.

Proposition One and ROC

These understandings of schools as white spaces and the ways in which processes that extend from them are thus racialized are important foundational ideas for my work. I offer the ROC framework as a way to further concretize the mechanisms schools use to replicate these ideals, and, more importantly, what the resultant implications are for Black and Latinx students. As a side note, I become profoundly angry when I think about these covert messages and the ways in which they operate in schools without acknowledgement. There is something deeply perverse about rigging a system to operate in a way that is traumatizing to Black and Latinx students and then blaming them for their condition. It is the ultimate form of gaslighting. Additionally, as established above, ideas about the role schools play in creating and perpetuating these racialized expectations are historically longstanding, which means that these harms are generationally propagated. Racial opportunity cost provides a lens through which to articulate these broader ideologies, providing a concrete structure for ideas that are purposefully difficult to see because they are so imbedded and interwoven into daily practice.

In the ROC framework, I collectively refer to these aspects of the institutional level operating in schools as *school factors* and break them into three categories. ***Climate factors*** relate to the environment that is created in a school and examine the norms and values that are established. An important aspect of that climate is also the opportunity to openly discuss racial issues and the racialized expectations that may be present as well as the sense of belonging that is cultivated. ***Structural factors*** examine places where we create inappropriate stratification in schools. This is primarily through tracking but can also occur through inappropriate special education and gifted placements, discipline disparities, and/or any other mechanisms that create separation in the school environment. ***Relationship factors*** highlight the importance of relationships with various stakeholders in the school building. The most critical relationship is with teachers, but this also includes principals, administrative assistants, and other adults on staff (custodial staff, food service workers, bus drivers, counselors, etc.). Students have hundreds of interactions with adults, all of which can serve to alleviate or exacerbate the ROC they experience. In figure 1 below, Proposition One appears at the top of the graphic and is labeled as "school factors." I expand on the nuances of each of these factors in chapter 1.

Proposition Two: Black and Latinx students navigate schools' dominant-normed expectations at a cost that must be understood and articulated

Having established from the research discussed in Proposition One the understanding of schools as racialized spaces and the resulting implications for all aspects of school life, the other important issue to untangle is what the implications are for Black and Latinx students. Students facing these racialized environments have three equally unfortunate choices. One, they can opt out of the game. Every educator I know has encountered racially minoritized students who are smart and could easily take on the challenges of more difficult coursework or earn higher grades but *choose* not to. My colleague Lance McCready and I coauthored a meta-nalysis of his research on Black and gender-nonconforming youths with my research on Black students in lower-track environments.[20] In that article, we explored how Black students with multiple minoritized identities were able to "make space" for themselves in ways that allowed them to survive and protect their well-being in the face of oppression, even if their behaviors did not always lead to academic success. They put themselves first, and this sadly put them at odds with the racialized expectations in their schools. While this population of students is not the primary focus of this book, this issue of course came up in discussions with research participants about other Black and Latinx students in their school and their thoughts on why they were not in their courses. To share just one example, one student, Carmen, talked about a friend who fit this description:

> There was this one guy who never took AP or pre-AP until like senior year. And he was just amazing, he aced everything. I knew him; he was a friend. He didn't care [in previous years], but then I guess he . . . I don't know. Something happened to him or something and he started [thinking about] his options for college. So, he went into the program. He was really brilliant.

Carmen was not the only student who referred to the fact that there were students who were perfectly capable of taking more advanced classes but chose not to, like this friend of hers who met this definition until he made a different choice. In this way, racial opportunity cost is likely to be useful in discussing the experiences of many Black and Latinx students, regardless of whether they have been seen as successful or realized what have been recognized as traditional markers of achievement. Thus, while this group of students is the focus of this book, it is incredibly important to acknowledge their existence as well as their understandable decision to prioritize their health and well-being by not engaging in the game.[21]

In accordance with existing research, those who do pursue traditional achievement benchmarks by enrolling in advanced course offerings or programs likely fall into one of two groups. One group follows what is perhaps the obvious path, aligning themselves closely with the white logics of their school environment, or what Carter termed an "achievement ideology."[22] In her research findings, students who fell into this category were identified as "cultural mainstreamers." In my previous research, I used a metaphor about driving to distinguish between two adaptation styles Black and Latinx students used to navigate the white logics they encountered in school.[23] The primary response that "mergers" took to navigating the racialized expectations in their school was to closely mirror those expectations, similar to Carter's cultural mainstreamers. However, as I and others have noted, students who align more closely with school expectations may find that they are taken further away from their home cultures. The glaring problem with schools being imbedded with white logics that students must negotiate in order to be successful in the eyes of the school is that they then exclude or denigrate the cultures of Black and Latinx students.

While perhaps a greater number of students fall into this category, they are also the students who likely experience the highest racial opportunity cost, like Ice or Rick, who will be introduced later in this book.

The final approach that students can take in response to the racialized expectations in their school is to push back against and navigate around them. Carter talked about students who adopted this approach as "cultural straddlers."[24] In my work, I have characterized students who use this as their primary navigation strategy as "weavers": they use code-switching and other tools to move in and out of the various expectations of the spaces they occupy at home, in school, and elsewhere. The challenge here is that while these students may have been more successful in remaining connected to their racial community compared to "mergers," the ability to choose this path was also connected to a school environment that was a bit more flexible in allowing students to bend, and/or the students themselves possessing individual characteristics that facilitated this path. Further, as even popular culture writers have noted, the ability to code-switch can exact its own toll.[25] In this way, the choice to adopt a "merger" or "weaver" navigation strategy was not entirely up to the students but was to some degree a reflection of the larger school environment.

Whatever approach students take in navigating the racialized expectations present in their schools, all are impacted by the challenge of doing so. Carter Andrews talked about this challenge of facing the "irreconcilable conflict" between expectations for a student's racial/ethnic group and those of the school.[26] Gibson discussed the challenge Punjabi Sikh students faced working to find "assimilation without accommodation" as they tried to align with the norms of the school without giving up too much of their cultural heritage.[27]

And, importantly, aligning with these dominant expectations still will not immunize students from conflict. Barajas and Pierce noted that the Latinas in their research achieved academic success but often at heavy "psychological price," or what Fordham has called a "pyrrhic victory," an idea originating in Roman times that refers to a battle that is technically won but inflicts such heavy losses it can hardly be considered a victory.[28] Carter and Tuitt noted the "atmospheric threats" students in their study encountered.[29] As previously noted, Valenzuela discussed the "subtractive" nature of schooling in her research with Mexican American students.[30] Indeed, the idea that success comes *at a cost* for racially minoritized students has been widely and painfully documented in existing research.

Proposition Two and ROC

ROC adds to this broader research on the experiences of racially minoritized students in white-normed schools a way of articulating the costs Black and Latinx students incur as a result of navigating the school factors identified in Proposition One. Racial opportunity costs (ROCs) fall into three broad categories: **Psychosocial costs** reflect the impact of navigating the racialized expectations on students' social–emotional and psychological well-being; **community costs** reflect the difficulty of maintaining a connection with friends, family, and members of the larger racial community; and **representation costs** reflect the responsibility of representing success for all members of their racial group, being put "on display" as ambassadors of diversity, and feeling a heightened sense of scrutiny in classroom and other school spaces. Proposition Two is represented at the bottom of the graphic in figure 1. The bidirectional arrows indicate the impact of school factors on the individual student, but also from the student to the institution/school to represent the potential for students to exert their own influence on the school environment. I take up these racial opportunity costs more substantively in chapter 2.

SUPPORTING PROPOSITIONS

I intentionally refer to the next two propositions as "supporting" to highlight an important understanding regarding the relationship among these four ideas. Propositions One and Two form the foundation of racial opportunity cost, which articulates the relationship between the school environment and its impact on the Black and Latinx students who navigate it. This relationship forms the heart of the ROC framework. However, two other considerations are important to understand in relation to these broader ideas. I have also referred to these supporting propositions as "mediating variables" as another way to talk about their relationship to school factors and ROC. This is useful phrasing because it highlights the ways in which these issues influence the broader relationship between Propositions One and Two—the rules that govern academic success and how those rules impact Black and Latinx students. One of these ways relates to other aspects of students' identities, in addition to race, that play a critical role in their experiences. The other addresses other influences on students' experiences in addition to the school (such as their family, their culture, or even themselves).

Supporting Proposition Three: Other aspects of Black and Latinx students' identities are important and must be acknowledged within the context of these broader institutional factors

Nearly thirty years ago, Cornel West published the seminal book "Race Matters."[31] The continued salience of race is an idea that forms the cornerstone of the position of critical race theorists, who, as mentioned earlier, broke from the critical legal theorists who preceded them in order to more substantively center race in their critique of the U.S. legal structure.[32] The continued importance of race notwithstanding, there are also profound and important ways that other aspects of identity matter. Famed scholar and critical race theorist Kimberlé Crenshaw advanced the notion of *intersectionality* to express the ways in which Black *women's* experiences are connected to both their race and gender identities (different from Black men or white women, for example).[33] There will always be a particular attention paid to the role of race in this country; however, it is also important to discuss how other social identities are also important for racially minoritized communities. The same is true for students navigating their racialized school environments, where their full complement of social identities are similarly relevant.

Earlier, I mentioned my collaboration with Dr. McCready, in which our students being "Black and" contributed to their experiences in important ways. Indeed, gender, gender identity, gender expression, and sexuality have long been acknowledged as important aspect of students' identities and thus their experiences in school.[34] Barajas and Pierce conducted research with Latinx students and the ways in which they pressed against traditional (white) conventions of assimilation.[35] An important finding from their work was that students' paths to success was deeply influenced by gender and the different (not necessarily better or worse) expectations and opportunities open to them as a result. It is critical that we pay more attention to the overlapping and mutually reinforcing impacts of students' various social identities. Findings from Jang's study with students with multiple minoritized identities (race, socioeconomic status, and sexual orientation) using a critical quantitative intersectionality framework reinforces the notion that these multiplicative identities are important to students' experiences.[36]

Supporting Proposition Three and ROC

I found that these same patterns from the broader literature about the salience of various social identities in addition to race were reflected in the stories shared by the Black and Latinx students who participated in this study. In terms of intersectional identities, it was clear that other identities mattered a great deal. These social identities included gender, social class, language, etc., but were always expressed in conversation with each other and particularly with respect to their racial identity(ies). Proposition Three is represented on the left side of the graphic in figure 1 and is referred to as "intersectional factors." Importantly, it is positioned on the side of the graphic to visually convey the idea that it is supportive to the primary relationship. Proposition Three is the subject of chapter 3.

Supporting Proposition Four: Individual, family, cultural, and other factors are important and must be acknowledged within the context of broader institutional factors

Another reason why beginning with an understanding of the role of the school, or institution, in creating the foundation for students' experiences in schools is important is because it was not acknowledged or considered for so long. Rather, traditional explanations focused on factors that began and ended with the student and perhaps their family. The seminal *Coleman Report*, published in 1966, highlighted these kinds of individual-level factors to the exclusion of school-level variables and cemented a generation of explanations that took its assertions as fact.[37]

In addition to being empirically false, these traditional explanations are deeply steeped in deficit thinking.[38] As noted by Valencia, at the core of deficit thinking lies the belief that if a student does not do well, it is because of internal factors: lack of intellectual ability or motivation, for example.[39] Deficit thinking is also connected to racist and culturally biased beliefs that label minoritized cultures as inferior.[40] The real problem with deficit thinking is that it lets us as educators off the hook for student performance, instead allowing us to blame the student for their situation. From this perspective, if students just cared more or tried harder, academic success would follow.

Examples of this kind of thinking are readily apparent across a variety of sources. One example comes from a book by Debbie Irving, who chronicles her journey to understand her white racial identity. Irving writes that she erroneously thought that she could be helpful to racially minoritized people by teaching them to be more like her.[41] She retained that perspective well into adulthood before taking a course on race in America that helped her begin to shift her perspective. I have met dozens of students like Irving, who mistakenly—but often so *earnestly*—believe that the most helpful thing they can do to help racially minoritized students is to teach them to assimilate into white logics. Another popular conversation has emerged about grit and resilience, which can also easily fall into deficit framings if not accompanied by structural critiques.

These deficit perspectives are still pervasive in schools and society today. Thus, we must be thoughtful about the ways in which we talk about other factors that play into students' experiences lest we inadvertently reinforce these negative stereotypes. Yes, of course, what people do matter; if a student does not study for a test, they are likely not to do well. There may also be important family or cultural factors that influence a student's situation. Further, there may be third-party actors that play a critical role in students' experiences, like community nonprofits or mentoring organizations. All of these factors absolutely matter. The point is that there is *so much more* that we do within the school environment that also matters and that significantly—and too often unfairly—influences students' experiences, particularly racially minoritized students. The good news is that we also have a substantial opportunity to positively impact students' experiences by addressing aspects of the school environment that are fully in our control as educators. The ROC framework is useful in helping teachers and school leaders concretely identify which aspects of the school environment to target.

Supporting Proposition Four and ROC

While the school will always be the primary factor in mediating students' experiences, these other aspects of a student's world also matter. It is important to consider how family can be an important source of support, or how individual aspects, such as resilience, also play a role in a student's ability to navigate the school environment, exacerbating or alleviating the ROC students experience. However, these factors must always

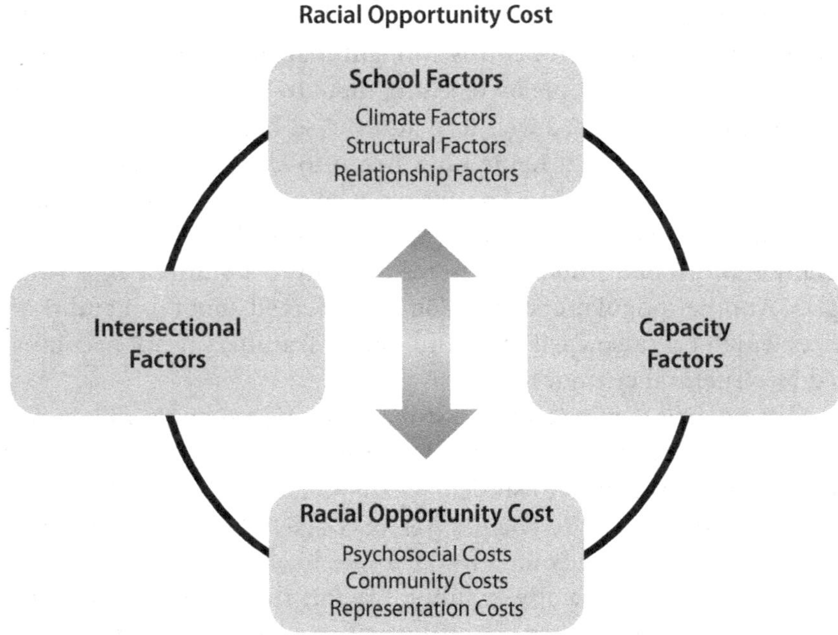

FIGURE 1 Racial Opportunity Cost

be considered in relation to the school environment, not separate from it. They influence a student's capacity to navigate the school environment. To that end, understanding the role of these non-school capacity factors (within the broader conversation about the larger institutional culture within which they occur) can help us better understand and thus address the racial opportunity cost students experience. I refer to these issues globally as *capacity factors*, as noted in figure 1 and address them more substantively in chapter 4.

CLOSING THOUGHTS ABOUT ROC

Ultimately, ROC fills an important conceptual and theoretical hole in our understanding of achievement, particularly as it relates to the experiences of racially minoritized students. Early in my career, I understood that we were missing nuanced language to talk about issues of achievement in a way that resonated with my personal and professional experience. The research existed and the scholarship had been established, but it had not been conceptualized in a way that reflected my experiences or the experiences of the students with whom I worked, especially the relationship between the school and how individual Black and Latinx students were influenced by that environment. Without that premise, the struggles racially minoritized students face can be seen at best as something that happens in isolation at particular schools; at worst, it sets up an opportunity for deficit thinking to encroach into explanations, suggesting that students of color should just work harder or that their families should care more.

I dive into the nuances of each of the ROC propositions and their relationship with various aspects of the ROC framework in chapters 1 through 4. And yet, these school factors, capacity factors, and intersectional factors work synergistically in ways that are important to understand with respect to the racial opportunity cost that a student experiences. Thus, in the concluding chapter, I spend some time exploring the connections across the various aspects of the ROC framework and offer additional thoughts about the potential broader utility of the ROC framework. While to this point I have used this framework to underscore the costs of success for high-achieving Black and Latinx students, I have always expected that it could be used to contextualize the experiences of other populations in school environments. This might include Black teachers or school leaders, or even other non-Black and Latinx racially minoritized students. I can also see this framework being used in non-K–12 school spaces, such as the experiences of Black people in the workforce or Latinx higher education faculty. The ROC framework may be useful in better understanding the costs that these individuals incur, and thus I devote some attention to these potential applications at the end of the book.

ABOUT THIS BOOK

I provide a more in-depth discussion of the research methods I used in this research project in the appendix, but I cannot move forward without providing at least an introduction to a few critical individuals: the graduate students who were part of my original research team and the eighteen students who participated in this project at two universities, "Northern College" and "Southern College" (pseudonyms, both). The research team was made up of me and three graduate students: one Black woman

(Rhonda Fowler) and two white women (Kristin Huggins and Leslie Locke). All three were in various stages of their doctoral programs at the time but are now university professors. Our time spent together was a highlight of the project; we drove to conduct interviews at Southern College a few different times and flew on a whirlwind visit to Northern College. When I refer in this book to the data collection we did together, I use the collective "we" to acknowledge their contributions. However, since this book is an independent project, I use the first person in the text when referring to choices that I have made.

I think I can speak for the team when I say how lucky we all felt to meet the young people who participated in the project. These were vibrant, intelligent students who were so open in sharing their stories with us; our conversations were often the first time they had been able to talk openly about these topics and so we tried very hard to put them at ease. At Southern College we talked with seven students: two Latinx students, Carmen (Hispanic) and Syril (Mexican), and five Black students: Gregg (African American), Jessica (African American), Melody (African American), Micayla (African American), and Rita (Black).[42] Eleven students participated from Northern College. One student, Rick, identified both as Black and Latinx (biracial: Puerto Rican/Black). Four students identified as Latinx at Northern College: Adriana (Latina), Araceli (Mexican American), Emma (Puerto Rican), and Lillie (Latina/Mexican). Six students identified as Black: Alexa (African American/Dominican), Carla (African American), Elsie (African American/Eritrean), Ice (African American), Moe (African American), and Zion (African American). We spoke with all of the students individually first to get to know them and their stories better; we then held focus groups with students of the same racial identity (Rick was given the choice of focus groups and opted for the Latinx group because it worked better with his schedule.)

Although over the years I have written a number of articles about racial opportunity cost, this book is specifically intended for practitioners. This framing is important to me because in my work as a professor, I have seen my students—often practicing teachers and school leaders themselves—struggle to understand some of the racial frameworks I have used in my classes. It can be difficult to make sense of white logics and the system of institutional racism that undergirds them in our daily practice. Thus, in this book, I frequently incorporate real-life examples. I have already started by discussing how deeply impacted I was by the events that unfolded in the aftermath of George Floyd's murder, including how a school district near my home chose to deal with the situation. I continue this trend by opening each chapter with a particular vignette that helps put the issues of focus for each chapter in sharp relief. In some cases, these vignettes are taken from news articles covering events that captured national attention. Other chapters begin with relevant popular-culture articles. Ultimately, these choices are intended to help reinforce the point that the issues that the students talk about in this book, and that the racial opportunity cost framework highlights, is something that is happening all around us in schools every day and that has influenced the lives of a significant number of people.

Regarding the ROC framework's broad applicability, between each chapter I include brief interludes, what I call "ROC Talks." These were penned by people close to this work, and close to me, and who provide an additional perspective on the ROC framework. These are people who speak to how the ROC framework explicates their own personal experiences. In other cases, they share how they have seen the framework working from their perspectives as practitioners. In all cases, they provide powerful testimony of the value of this work.

I also want to share a few thoughts about terminology. I use the terms Black, Latinx, and racially minoritized fairly consistently through the text; however, I acknowledge and appreciate that students have a wide range of preferences in terms of identity. Thus, when speaking about a specific student, I try to use their preferred racial identity. Their self-described identities are also included in the participant profiles in Appendix B. In keeping with my own longstanding preferences, but happily also ever-progressing editorial conventions, I choose to capitalize Black but not white.[43] I also acknowledge that the pan-ethnic term *Latinx* has its own history and controversy.[44] I use the term Latinx in deference to its broader gender neutrality but acknowledge that the term may not be broadly reflective of the preferences of the U.S. Latinx community. Ultimately, no one term is universally representative, and so I offer these explanations for why I have settled on particular selections and respect that others might have chosen differently.

Here is one last thought about my use of the term "racial opportunity cost," or ROC. I use this term two ways throughout the book. As a concept, I may refer to a "student's ROC" or talk about the "ROC" that students experience. However, I also use it as a framework, which is clearly spelled out in figure 1 and further elucidated in chapters 1 through 4. In the latter, each element of the ROC framework includes additional nuance and structure that together represent the theoretical contribution. Both applications and uses—concept and theory—are correct.

CHAPTER 1

School Factors[1]

A LETTER SENT HOME TO PARENTS BY A PRINCIPAL IN HOUSTON, Texas, went viral in April 2019 because of what many felt were extreme restrictions on the attire that *parents* could wear on school grounds or while attending school events on and off school property.[2] Leggings, ripped jeans, tank tops, hair wraps, and bonnets were all flagged on the offensive list. In explanation, the principal wrote:

> Parents, we do value you as a partner in your child's education. You are your child's first teacher. However, please know we have to have standards, most of all we must have high standards. We are preparing your child for a prosperous future. We want them to know what is appropriate and what is not appropriate for any setting they may be in. This is a professional educational environment where we are teaching our children what is right and what is correct or not correct.

The letter, provided in English and Spanish, was sent home to all parents. I share this story for two reasons. First, it is an explicit example of the ways in which expectations are tied to success. In her letter, the principal connected having a "prosperous future" to whether a person wore rollers in their hair in public. Every few months, we hear a news report about a school receiving criticism because of its dress code: these stories invariably involve Black children being scrutinized for their hair style, wearing a hoodie, or some other innocuous style choice. Though perhaps shocking, these kinds of rules are not unusual—we hear about them with some frequency. Rather, what is uncommon is when schools have codified these rules so explicitly in formal policy. That is, they *talked* about them. Typically, these expectations would remain part of the hidden curriculum. This is one reason why I chose to share this story.

A second reason I chose to share this story stems from the demographics of the school where the incident took place. We might not expect a school with a Black principal and a student population that is 99 percent Black and Latinx to espouse these kinds of racialized performative expectations, perhaps anticipating them instead in predominantly white schools. And, of course, these examples come from those schools, too. This story underscores the point that these racialized expectations transcend demographic and geographic considerations. Indeed, they are imbedded in the structures and norms of our entire educational system, from teacher and leadership education programs, to systems of state and federal school finance, to legacies of residential segregation, and so on. Thus, despite the fact that this Houston school probably had only a handful of white students, it was still imbued with the same performative expectations that were based on the white logics that characterize the entire U.S. educational system, regardless of local demographics.

SCHOOL FACTORS AND ROC

Understanding the context within which Black and Latinx students operate is critical to recognizing their racial opportunity cost because it helps us appropriately consider the behaviors and decisions they make. Without that awareness, our perspective would be incomplete. We might also be doomed to replicate the deficit thinking that unfairly holds students to blame for the challenges they encounter. Centering this systemic perspective is important is because it is an aspect of how schools operate that is not well understood. Many students do not see how the challenges they face stem from these institutionalized processes. They are not taught to see these processes. Many educators do not see them and thus do not teach about them because they were not taught to see them, either.

I structure school factors into three categories: ***climate factors*** address the overall culture or environment of the school.[3] ***Structural factors*** examine places where we create inappropriate segregation through tracking or any other mechanism that results in stratification, like disproportionate special education or gifted placements, or discipline disparities. Finally, ***relationship factors*** highlight the importance of relationships with various stakeholders in the building. This obviously includes teachers, but also school leaders and other staff (custodial staff, food service workers, bus drivers, counselors, etc.). In this chapter, I will use these three broad categories to structure a conversation about the role of the school in creating environments that can alleviate but too often exacerbate the racial opportunity cost (ROC) that students experience.

CLIMATE FACTORS

Climate factors are most connected to the ideas reflected in the story that started this chapter. While the principal's letter was about the dress code specifically, educators know that each school community has a sense of "how things work here"—formal and informal rules of operation, if you will. Understanding the ways in which racialized expectations influence the climate and culture of a school environment is the first school factor to understand. Not only must Black and Latinx students work hard to be successful, but they must be successful *in the way the school expects.* I categorize climate factors into three areas: the norms and values that are promoted, the discussions of race and racism that are fostered, and the sense of belonging that is cultivated.

Promoting open school norms and values

The students with whom we spoke helped us understand the nuances of the expectations in their own school environments. However, connected to my earlier point about students not being taught to see or understand these larger racialized expectations, our conversations with students about these issues were often long and windy. These were not topics that they had had the space to talk about before and thus were deliberate and thoughtful in finding the words to describe what they had experienced. Carla, an African American woman who grew up in Chicago, had noted some patterns in how students at her school formed groups:

> I know a lot of the white students in my classes were mostly from the same background. They were all from the same neighborhood. It was kinda like middle class, like maybe upper middle class. And they all hung out together and thought the same way. I don't feel like there was much diversity or people challenging that. And a lot of us [Black students], too, we were of the same group.

What was interesting in Carla's comment was that while she noted that these students were all in the same classes together, she did not talk about similarities in academic ability. Rather, the connection she saw was in their socioeconomic background, the neighborhoods in which they lived, and the similar kind of thinking they displayed. She extended this same sense of separateness to the other Black students, which she also saw as "of the same group." I took this to mean that she saw this group of Black students who were with her in advanced classes as both separate from the white students in those classes, but potentially also separate from other Black students in the school.

Sometimes, we found that students had internalized deficit explanations for the racialized disparities they witnessed. For example, Zion was an insightful young man who had a unique perspective on his schooling experiences because he had been forced to leave his small, predominantly Black elite private high school in New Orleans for a year in the aftermath of Hurricane Katrina. He could not help but notice the racial disparities in his new school. When we asked him to reflect on what the causes of those disparities might be, like Carla, he spoke not to differences in academic ability, but in performative differences between Black and white students.

> I think it's just because the Black students acted very different than what they were supposed to act. Like, how they were *supposed* to act.

Zion noticed that Black students at his new school were not seen to fit in with the school's expectations for success. But I noticed some deficit thinking creeping in here when he seemed to assign the responsibility to the students—*they* did not act the way they were supposed to act. But when he emphasized "supposed" to act, he was hinting at those expectations. As we talked with him in his interview, it became clear to me that he did not truly believe that Black students were inherently worse behaved than other students, but it was the explanation that he had learned. I chose to highlight Zion and Carla here, but many students made similar assertions in our conversations with them.

However, sometimes students took their analysis a step further, demonstrating that they had also started to make connections about the rules in place in their schools. For example, in his interview, Ice also talked about the messages his school tried to instill in him:

> With the people I know around home, some of their schools make them feel like what they were giving up was something they should give up in the first place. Like, not necessarily that it was much of a choice [about] what you want to do. But it was like, "You should give up where you come from, anyway." Like, "That's not what you should be looking at," you know. Like, "Don't worry about that—what's back there. You can do something better. You *should* do something better. And what you want to do," you know, like be a doctor or a lawyer or whatever, "is better than being a mechanic or being somebody who knows a mechanic. Don't settle for people like that."

> Terah: Do you think that message is true? Like, that they should?
>
> Ice: Oh! Do I think I agree with them? No. No, no, no. . . . Like what they're saying turn your back on, seriously, was home. And I don't agree with that. I mean, you gotta get out of home at some point, but I don't think turning your back on home is necessary to get out.
>
> Terah: So, you think some schools make that a dichotomy? Like, you either leave or you stay and that's—
>
> Ice: —the ultimate choice.

Ice was one of the students for whom the concept of racial opportunity cost particularly resonated. Ice was open with us about the messages he received from his school that told him what he should strive for if he wanted to be successful: that pursuing a more so-called prestigious career like doctor or lawyer was preferred *and* that it would be appropriate to leave his family behind to do so. You "leave or you stay" and that is the "ultimate choice" for a student to make. Ice was conflicted about these messages. He did not feel that he should have to leave his family behind. In fact, he was adamant in his opposition to the idea that a student should have to leave their family behind in order to meet these expectations. Nonetheless, he still felt his school expected him to do just that if he wanted to be successful.

Ice's story made clear that his school had established expectations that he would need to follow if he wanted to do well, but he was not as explicit at this point in the interview about the role race played in those expectations. However, Alexa was. When we spoke with her, she shared an exchange that she had had with a teacher after learning that another teacher had told his students, "Fine. Don't listen. All of you can get in line for your welfare checks." In the aftermath of the incident, she told us about the conversation she had had with her teacher about what had happened:

> I was like, "Well, [the teacher who made the comment] treated me perfectly fine." And she's like, "That's because you fit into the white category." And so like, because of, uh, because of the way they view me, they would never, like, I would never be put into that situation.

Alexa struggled to express what she experienced in this situation, starting and stopping her sentences, clearly uncomfortable with the idea that she was seen differently from other Black students. However, her story revealed that her teacher was also aware of the racial implications of the incident and how Alexa was seen in the school. Ironically, perhaps, the teacher who made the comment that triggered the situation was Black and the teacher with whom she talked about it was white. This may seem counterintuitive but in fact supports the point that these racialized expectations are deeper than how an individual person identifies or what they may believe. We are all, every one of us, caught up in the racial logics that operate in society. That explains why a Black teacher can be an agent in the perpetuation of deficit thinking and the institutionalized racism that feeds it. Without intervention, we all learn and internalize these racialized expectations when we are young, we perpetuate them in our interactions as we age, and we often do not even know we are doing it. It is devastating when we see examples like this one, where a racially minoritized person like the teacher in Alexa's story has internalized these racial logics and propagates them, but it is not surprising. It is merely confirming evidence that we must keep our attention focused on what is happening at the institutional level and analyze the actions of individuals within that larger framework.

There are numerous examples from the students we talked with of encounters—or, more often, conflicts—with these kinds of racialized expectations in their schools. For example, Carmen confronted this when she came in first in her school's academic rankings and a student expressed surprise that she could have achieved this status.

> I was first in the class. And it was this big surprise because I didn't really know anything about rank.... One of my friends told me this sometime later that there was this one girl that said that, how could I be first, that I was Mexican. That didn't make sense to her.

Like the Black teacher Alexa mentioned, the student Carmen referenced had similarly internalized the racial logics in the school. Although much younger than Alexa's teacher, this student, who, like Carmen, also identified as Mexican, had already learned the lesson that Mexican students were not *supposed* to excel academically in the way that Carmen had. It "didn't make sense" to her that Carmen was ranked first. In our conversations with students, we heard story after story of how these Black and Latinx students were reminded that they did not fit into the mold of how racially minoritized students were expected to act, dress, or speak.

The stories that Alexa and Carmen shared referenced incidents that had happened in high school, but students also encountered situations in college where they faced these racial logics and were reminded that their being successful did not match the expected scripts. Syril, another Mexican American student, told us about an incident that had happened when he met a new person off campus while he was a student at Southern College:

> She's like, "So what school do you go to?" And I'm like, "Oh, [Southern College]. She's like, "Really?" And she flat out told me, "Wow, you look dumber than that." [Interviewers express shock]. Yeah, she said it straight to my face. Well, that's good though 'cause I like to be able to prove you wrong when you ask me stuff like that, you know?

This person had just met Syril and thus had no foundation to judge him other than his appearance. Her comment that Syril "looked dumb" makes sense when filtered through racial logics that tell us that smart people are white. Sadly, though hardly surprising, this brown-skinned man did not match what she had learned "smart" people who could attend an elite school like Southern College should be.

While most of the students talked about the ways in which racialized expectations influenced their experiences, they of course felt the impact of those expectations in different ways. For example, Gregg pushed back against the idea that he needed to assimilate into the white-normed culture of his high school:

> No, I bent it to me. I bent it to me as best I can. I'm a truly independent person. I said, "I'm not changing myself to make you feel better."

Gregg's experiences stood apart from many of the students we talked with, primarily because his status as an athlete as well as his unique personal characteristics allowed him to navigate his school's expectations according to his own rules. Micayla espoused a similar perspective. Like Gregg, when we asked her if she ever had to modify or suppress aspects of her identity in order to better meet the expectations of her high school, she told us:

> I felt like I always fit the mold academically. And I guess, as long as you can fit it academically, you would be successful. That was the most important thing. As long as you made the grade. Since I was able to make the grade and I was able to keep up, that was basically the only way I fit the mold. I was really kind of separate from that whole [white-normed] culture.

Micayla made a compelling point here. Like Gregg, she fell into the category of "weaver"—those students who were better able to move in and out of various contexts, mirroring the expectations of each to fit in. From that perspective, she did have an easier time "fitting the mold" and being successful. However, unlike Gregg, who stood as an exception, there were aspects of Micayla's experience that require some unpacking. Similar to many of the students we talked with, Micayla was uncomfortable with even the suggestion that she had to compromise who she was in order to be successful. In this way, her perspective was similar to Ice's, who was also adamant that he did not *want* to align with the performative scripts in his school but did so because he felt there was no other choice if he wanted to be successful. Relatedly, Micayla was adamant about expressing her full identity in the spaces she entered but also shared many stories that confirmed that doing so nonetheless influenced how she was seen and treated. Carmen shared an analogous perspective about not feeling compelled to act differently in her classes:

> I never felt like I had to change who I was. Because even throughout the whole thing, I didn't share [white students'] music tastes. I didn't listen to their music. I spoke Spanish when I wanted to.... I never changed who I was because I wanted to fit in.

Carmen felt confident to be herself in school, not feeling pressure to change her musical tastes or to not speak Spanish. Importantly, taking this approach did not hold her back academically, as she ranked first in her class. The juxtaposition of her perspective with the broader school context is interesting, though: although Carmen felt like she did not have to fit a particular mold, *other* Mexican American students felt like they did (and perhaps also felt that Carmen should) as evidenced by the student who questioned her ranking.

The stories shared in this section reveal two important points about the climate cultivated in their schools around achievement. The stories shared by Zion, Carla, Alexa, and Ice establish the first point: their experience with racialized expectations for their actions, dress, and behavior. They shared specific examples of their encounters with or reminders of their schools' white logics. Importantly, even as some students were aware of these racialized expectations, it was clear that they were not in agreement with them or comfortable with the idea that they would have to make accommodations to align with them, like Ice and Micayla. The second point is that even for those students who told us that they did not feel compelled to change aspects of their behavior in order to be successful, like Micayla, Carmen, and Gregg, their ability or decision to do so said more about their individual circumstances than it did the overall school climate. For example, as we will discuss later, Micayla shared several stories about the pressures she felt to represent for Black students in her relatively white advanced placement courses. Additionally, we know from other students with whom Carmen was acquainted that they at least felt pressured to conform in certain ways. Even Gregg, who perhaps experienced the most freedom of expression, was clear that few other Black students in his school were able to achieve what he did. This issue of individual characteristics is an important but complicated aspect of the students' experiences to unpack and will be more fully explored in chapter four.

Fostering open discussion of race and racism

Another key aspect of climate factors is the opportunity to talk about race and racism in an open, comfortable environment—or, more often, how *not* having that chance created challenges for the Black and Latinx with whom we spoke. One of the challenges with understanding what these students faced in their school environments was that the hurdles were largely invisible. These white logics were purposefully difficult to see; we can see their consequences, but that only makes it easier to misassign blame to other easier targets (like Zion, whose initial explanation for racial disparities was to suggest that Black students acted differently from how they were supposed to act). This is why having open conversations about race but also the deeper racialized structures with which schools and society are imbued is important for students so that they are not left to internalize the blame themselves, or, worse, believe that they come from families or cultures that are just not achievement oriented. A critical first step toward that goal then is to just start talking about it. Unfortunately, across the conversations we had with students, most indicated having very little opportunity to even do that. Carla spoke about this when she said, "We didn't really talk about race that much." Or Lillie, who said:

> We didn't even discuss race in our school. We never discussed race at all. It wasn't a thing that we did; I don't know why.

The stories that Carla and Lillie shared were fairly reflective of what most of the students experienced in their high schools, which was very little opportunity to openly or proactively address racial issues. Some students had access to student-led groups in their school—perhaps a culture club or some other racial affinity group—where they addressed these issues. However, while the existence of such clubs was important, they did not take the place of official school-sponsored opportunities to talk about these issues. The overall absence of school cultures in which opportunities for racial dialogue were cultivated made the experiences that much more exceptional when they occurred. Zion confirmed that he also lacked the broader opportunity to substantively talk about race but did have one teacher who took on the issue regularly. Talking about the impact of this teacher, he said:

> That was the only class we ever had an open discussion about race. You could say what you wanted or what you thought. People were actually honest. I didn't really think that was gonna happen. [Laughs] Yeah, people usually hold back. I always appreciate it when people are honest about race. 'Cause, how else are you supposed to figure things out?

Zion's question was central. How *are* students supposed to figure things out if there are no opportunities to talk about race? He recalled fondly the environment that his teacher created to talk about these issues and to share honestly about their feelings. He cherished this experience, but it also made him realize how much he was missing out on in other classes that were not so open. Given what we know about the hidden curriculum and how these various rules are purposely hidden, it is imperative that we talk about them. Indeed, Lisa Delpit talked about the importance of teaching and talking about them as one of her rules of the culture of power.

I want to highlight two particularly poignant stories that speak to the consequences of students not having the opportunity to talk about race in their schools. The first is from Moe, a Black student at Northern College who reminded us that race did not cease to be relevant or present just because it was not addressed substantively. Indeed, racial issues emerged with relative frequency, which only made for awkward interactions. Moe told us that in class one day a teacher had said, "Black people are like 'this.' Am I right, Moe?" Moe was like, "What?" Moe's teacher then went on to say, "I mean, like, you're Black, but you're not *that* Black." As I reflected on Moe's story, I thought about the position so many students are put in to represent "the" Black experience, a terrible situation for Moe made worse by the racial stereotyping that he was being asked to validate. This teacher reminded me of the kindergarten teacher from Hatt's research, where over the course of the year in which she studied the classroom, students were taught that "smart" kids are white. The teacher's comments to Moe and the rest of the class were an opportunity to reinforce those dangerous racial logics. Sadly, these were not isolated incidents; there are numerous opportunities every day for these kinds of racialized scripts to be reconfirmed for students. Not talking about it only makes the situation worse because they are then normalized even further.

Like Moe, Rick attended a school where racial incidents were swept under the rug. Not talking about racial issues openly was also not a winning strategy for avoiding racial conflict in his private Catholic school for young men. Several racist incidents transpired during his tenure at the school. The first was a racial slur that had been written on another Black student's locker when Rick was a sophomore. School officials gathered Black students together after the incident occurred, assuring them, Rick said, that they were "gonna handle it" and that they were "doing the most that [they could]." However, according to Rick, very little changed in the school after that incident. Apparently, staff hoped the problem would just go away on its own. Unfortunately, two years later, there was another racist incident. This time, the school was able to identify the perpetrator, who was disciplined. However, there was no discussion of what happened, no recognition of the pattern of behaviors that might have suggested a larger racial problem in the school. Rick was even more upset after the second incident because of the school's lack of substantive response:

> I felt kind of a little bit offended, maybe because they didn't give us an invitation to figure out what was going on. Because this was something that we had been through before. And the victim of the sophomore incident, he just shook his head. He was just saying, "Stuff happened again. It's never gonna change." So, that had a lot to do with the whole Black mentality at my school, especially like kinda checking out. Like, "This is not supportive for us." And because [I'm] multicultural, it was kinda my mission to bring it up, in a sense. But I did get some flak (for bringing it up). It was like, "Why are we talking about this? What's the purpose?" Like, "It's not gonna change anything. Why do we always have to talk about race? Why does it have to be about Black and white? Why can't we all just get along?"

Rick had already told us that there were no Black or Latinx teachers or administrators at his school. It likely never crossed their mind that Black students might feel targeted or that there was an issue with the culture of their school. Rick reported feeling a responsibility to raise concerns about what happened because he was Black and Puerto Rican, although this should not have been a burden he was expected to carry. Further exacerbating the situation were the white students who suggested Rick should not have raised the issue in the first place. They could not understand why he wanted these things to be talked about because there was no precedent for it. Ironically, they wanted to know why they "always have to talk about race" even though they literally never did talk about it. Nonetheless, they had a perceived fatigue about it perhaps because they were used to racist issues *happening* and mistook that for actual discussions. This experience caused Rick to feel even more isolated in his school climate: not only were these issues ignored, but he was made to feel like he was wrong for wanting them to be addressed.

Across the conversations we had with students emerged an understanding of the true wrong being inflicted upon these students by not having the opportunity to talk about race in their schools. Thus, talking about race emerged as an important aspect of climate factors because it was such a critical aspect of the overall culture of the school. Just because a school ignored racial issues did not make them go away. Ignoring these issues had the further isolating effect of making racially minoritized students' experiences worse. Trust in their teachers and school leaders was eroded, and the racial opportunity cost they experienced was exacerbated.

Cultivating a sense of belonging and community

More and more evidence is surfacing about the importance of building community in schools.[4] To demonstrate the importance of belonging and community for the students with whom we spoke, I chose to focus on one student's story and the way that a simple incident in class compromised his sense of belonging and engagement rather than share multiple examples. Zion told us about a teacher who used sailing to demonstrate a concept in class one day. Whatever the subject was, the focus was not on sailing, and knowledge of boating was not required. So when the teacher demonstrated the concept using sailing as a metaphor, it set off a spiral of doubts for Zion:

> I was like [to myself], "I really don't know what you're talking about at all. I never even tried [sailing] in my entire life. . . ." I couldn't be the only one raisin' my hand in class, "I don't get the boat thing. Could you explain that again, like change it up a little?" So, I think you really see why it doesn't work, or why it's not the way it should be. Because they cater to the middle, upper white class in everything they do: the way they explain things, the way they expect you to understand things, and all that. So, I think that's why some of the Black students just don't get it, and then they start falling behind. And [the teachers] just take that as them not knowing or not being as smart, which sucks.

There's so much here to unpack from Zion's poignant point. In the same way that he started to extrapolate about how another student may have been impacted by the situation, I imagine the potential implications of his experience in class that day. First, he felt that because the teacher used sailing as an example, he was supposed to know about sailing. No one else asked for clarification, which only reinforced to him that it was something he should know about. Hearing his story, I remember thinking that there were surely other students who had also never been sailing but who were reticent to say that they had not. But whether or not other children were confused is not the point, because at the time, Zion took the absence of other students asking questions to mean that they *did* know.

Second, because no one else asked questions, Zion felt that meant sailing was something he was *supposed* to know about. The thought of not knowing something he should have known sent him down another spiral of self-doubt. As the only Black student in the class, he certainly was not then going to raise his hand and single himself out for not knowing—not if he thought he was the only one in the course who did not understand sailing. Third, and this is where I think things take a particularly devastating turn, is that he did not learn whatever concept the sailing metaphor was supposed to teach him. We can only speculate, but perhaps he did not learn the concept and so really did start to fall behind. He lost his confidence. And perhaps he would be less willing to ask questions about other concepts because he had begun to believe that he just did not understand the material. He thus did not learn other concepts in the class. And, as his grades started to fall, feelings that maybe he was not supposed to be in that class would likely start to rise.

Fourth, as Zion pointed out, the teacher may not have realized that his slip in performance actually stemmed from an easily remedied issue. The teacher may have believed that—like other racially minoritized students who had taken the course and struggled (perhaps with similar issues around cultural bias in the curriculum)—he was just not going to be successful. She would give up without ever really trying. A teacher may see a student's lack of engagement in the class and subsequent poor performance on a test and take that as confirming evidence that racially minoritized students just do not do well in the course; not because they cannot be successful, but because the material is culturally biased. Fifth, the student may shy away from taking additional classes like that one, either because they thought the coursework was too challenging or perhaps because the pressure of being the only racially minoritized student in the class was too much. Teachers of those classes perhaps do not encourage students to take other challenging classes because their teacher has already spread the word about the student's struggles. While aspects of this somewhat fictionalized extension of the story that Zion shared may seem extreme, it demonstrates the ways in which a lack of belonging can really impede pathways to success.

One other issue that is important to point out in cultivating a sense of belonging and engagement is that a sense of belonging does not mean students need to be in racially heterogenous environments all the time. It is appropriate and even necessary for racially minoritized students to be in spaces where they are just around other Black and Latinx students. Indeed, this is a common occurrence for most white students; being in racially homogenous environments is relatively commonplace for them. The point is that *both* kinds of spaces are needed—spaces (and teacher and school leader *support* for spaces) that allow Black and Latinx students to talk about their experiences, to learn about topics that are relevant to them, and to experience joy. And, of course, they need racially diverse classrooms at all levels where they can have those experiences, too. Both racially homogeneous and heterogeneous spaces are important for a robust and healthy sense of belonging for all students.

Ultimately, the climate established in a school was the most important in the ROC that students experienced because it established the baseline from which everything else stemmed. One aspect of school climate is the general norms and values that are cultivated in the school: What scripts are upheld to which students are expected to aspire? Further, how open are teachers and school leaders about racial issues and the inner workings of white logics? Finally, how well are we doing at fostering students' sense of belonging and engagement? Each of these is a critical aspect of school climate that must be better understood.

STRUCTURAL FACTORS

When I was conducting previous research on the implications of tracking for Black students, I spent quite a bit of time just sitting in math and English classes, following students through their daily schedules and generally getting to know the focal students in my project. We were probably about a month into my observations in the school when I held my first focus group with the students. I had developed a pretty good rapport with each of them by then. In addition to conducting multiple hours of observations with each student, I had also interviewed all seven of them, individually, several times. These were animated, vocal, energetic teens. And yet, as they walked into the classroom the afternoon of our first focus group, they were as quiet as I'd ever seen them. "You all are acting like you've never even seen each other before!" I said, trying to break the awkward silence that had descended on the group as we waited to officially get started.

As the words left my mouth, I realized that was exactly what was going on. These kids *did not* know each other. Well, the students in the alternative- and regular-track classes knew each other. However, adding the students who were taking advanced classes to the mix changed the dynamic. This experience was actually a good example of how seemingly neutral processes and practices can become biased against racially minoritized students. There is an art to master class scheduling: deciding which classes to offer while balancing school capacity with student demand. If an assistant principal has a group of twelfth graders who are interested in taking both AP Government and AP World History one term, those courses cannot be offered at the same time. As a result of making that accommodation, though, sometimes these students may also by default get put into the same lunch period and/or gym class. Although it may seem a bit odd to think of a group of students in what may be seen as "AP Gym," it might not seem problematic to solve a scheduling issue in this manner. However, there are many concerns with this solution, one of which is the broader problem of catering to high-achieving students when building master schedules. In terms of ROC, however, the issue is that because of the white logics that permeate schools and push students from racially minoritized backgrounds out of more rigorous coursework, the few Black and Latinx students who take advanced classes may not then have *any* other courses with other racially minoritized students—not even lunch.

Looking at the kids around the table at the focus group and reflecting on my experiences with them, I realized I *knew* they did not have classes together. I had sat through a number of full-day schedules with each of them by that point. Darica and Cortez, students in the alternative-track program, sometimes had classes together because the program was so small. Other than that, I had never sat in a class with two of the participants. As I thought further about the interviews I had conducted with them up to that point, I had another realization. Many of the kids had been in the same district since elementary school but had not had meaningful classes together since then. The separation that they had experienced over many years ended up being a significant theme in my research. The tension I felt as the students came into the classroom soon eased, and it was not long before they started becoming more acquainted with one another, cracking jokes and sharing stories. By the end of the research project, they had learned a lot from each other, and I hoped they would continue their friendships.

When I started the project on racial opportunity cost, then, I made sure to ask the students about their experiences with tracking and other forms of stratification and separation. Not surprisingly, it emerged as a significant factor in many of the students' experiences. Students who had taken advanced classes—an overwhelming majority of the study participants—surely were exposed to a more challenging curriculum that helped prepare them for the rigorous expectations of their elite college environments. However, that preparation came *at a cost.* The tracking and ability grouping theme was also the only one where I found no positive examples. With all the other school factors, while there were certainly ways that policies and practices exacerbated students' racial opportunity cost, there were also examples of a positive impact—even if they were isolated to particular classrooms or teachers. This was not the case in our conversations about tracking. All the experiences the students shared were negative; tracking did not help them nor provide any advantage that they could identify.

The example of master scheduling that I shared above demonstrates how even classes like gym and art can end up with a disproportionate number of the same students who are taking other advanced classes together. Thankfully, the students in our project did not have such extreme experiences. Jessica did say that her interactions with other Black students were limited because of racialized tracking, however:

> We only got to take like art or P.E. with other [Black] people. So, I really didn't have like a chance to interact with many of the other Black students a lot. We were kinda segregated.

Jessica did not have much interaction with other Black students because the advanced courses she took were predominantly white. Outside of classes like gym, which were not separated by ability, she felt segregated from other Black students.

One of the justifications school leaders sometimes offer about tracking is the choice students have to enroll in whatever classes they would like. They maintain that they do not have tracking because they do not directly lock students into particular levels or groupings. While this may be true in theory, Zion talked about how in practice, his preferences had relatively little impact on his options.

> I went through like the regular track for my first two years. And then they saw that I was smarter than that. So they switched me over to honors my junior year. And then, 'cause it's hard to switch over or whatever 'cause your schedule just gets all messed up, they have to use some classes you can't take with [your new schedule]. Especially with the math classes. They can't just put you in honors because you haven't taken, like, a class a year ahead of you. So, I was in regular math classes still.

Teachers saw potential in Zion to take more rigorous classes, so after the first two years, his schedule shifted. But this was not a normal occurrence, and he talked about how difficult it was to achieve this course change because of all the scheduling consequences. However, again, because students who are in one advanced class are usually taking several advanced classes, taking a non-advanced math class made it hard to create his schedule. Thus, in effect, students in Zion's school were tracked, it just happened indirectly as a by-product of scheduling constraints. Zion did not just talk about the difficulty with scheduling but commented on the different expectations between his regular and honors courses.

> It was weird 'cause like regular classes are so much different than the honors classes were. Yeah. 'Cause regular class is like a bunch a football players and like a bunch a football coaches teaching it. And it was like fake classes, basically. [Interviewer asks what he means by fake classes.] They were just like, "Do whatever. Just like, pretend to do your real work, and like you'll get by." 'Cause they didn't wanna like hurt the football players too much. Yeah. So, it was like fake classes. Some of the classes were real. Like, my English freshmen year was a good class. English sophomore year was like not even.

Zion's point was that his honors classes were not just more challenging, but he also felt that his honors teachers were more invested in him. They seemed to care more about him as a person. The experience gave him the perspective that the regular classes were "fake" because he felt they were not really intended to teach anything. Students in regular classes were expected to just "get by" in those classes so that they would not be impeded from playing football.

Zion's point about the regular track classes having low expectations was a point that Micayla raised, as well. Although she did not take those courses, she remained close with other Black students who did. She told us,

> You had a few Black people in the [international baccalaureate] IB program, and we were always stressed out. And then all of our friends who weren't doing IB classes, they didn't even bring books to school. It was just ridiculous. The gap between the level of work we were doing and the level of work they were doing was just like a gigantic gap. . . . [My school] was like prison. And it was basically like, "Just get them [regular-track students] in class. Keep them out the hallways." You know? "Keep them in line." It was really just like, "Keep them from going crazy" instead of trying to educate them.

Micayla picked up the same point Zion did that the regular classes were meant to get the students who were enrolled in them out of the way of the students in the IB program, which was the population to whom the school primarily catered. She even compared her school to prison in terms of cultivating a significant separation between IB students and all the others. Both Zion and Micayla told us that the difference between the regular and advanced classes were not just about rigor, but were opportunities to reinforce the racial logics that suggested that racially minoritized students were not as important and thus the schools did not have to bother with them. Micayla referred to it as prison; Zion called the classes fake. Neither characterization was positive.

Zion and Micayla addressed the experience of tracking from the perspective of students, but Rita added another dimension to the issue by discussing the teachers' roles in reinforcing messages to students about their track placement. She told us:

> Schools . . . [should not] make such a distance between students on the regular track and the honors track. Teachers are like, "Oh, look at them. Look at what they're doing with their lives." And like, "You should be like them, and da da." All that does is tell the other students like, "You suck. What's wrong with you? Why can't you get right?"

> These are people they've been with since elementary school. It gets worse and worse, and teachers manifest that. . . . That's one of the big reasons why students in the regular track feel like they can't cross over—or they don't want to—and why [high-track] students feel like they're giving up so much. Because they're being told that they're different, and they can't really come back to where everybody else is.

Rita raised a number of critical points in her response to us: her point that students who were taking less-advanced classes were supposedly not doing anything meaningful with their lives was a reflection of the racial logic that teachers were perpetuating. I also appreciated Rita's point that these students sometimes *choose* not to take more-advanced classes because they feel they have to give up so much—or, that the perceived racial opportunity cost was too high. She noted, like Micayla and Zion did, that students in those advanced classes were not only provided with a superior education, but they were also catered to and supported in ways that students in less-advanced classes were not. The teachers helped manifest that separation by reinforcing the idea that the students in higher level classes were *better* than the students who were not in those classes. Thus, track placements were not simply a function of ability or an opportunity to be further challenged, they were a primary mechanism in reinforcing and perpetuating racial logics and the broader system of institutional racism that they fueled.

I saw these kinds of double standards myself during my observations of tracked classrooms in my previous research. One day, a (white) student in an AP English class threw his desk across the room because his (white) teacher had taken away his phone after repeated reminders—on that day and on several previous occasions when I had been observing the class—that having a phone out where she could see it was against the rules. His teacher actually apologized to him for making him upset. Earlier the same day, I had sat through a mind-numbing first period regular English class in which the teacher spent the first 35 minutes of a 50-minute class literally waiting until every person in the class had their book open on the same page with their attention focused "properly" on her before beginning the lesson. I vividly remember how slowly the minutes of that particular class ticked by, and I was not even a student! I have no recollection of the lesson she taught. These experiences—those that the students in the ROC project shared as well as my own from observations of tracked classrooms—reinforced what we already know from existing research. These stratified classrooms are not about supporting individual learning differences but are too often about control and propagating racialized expectations in the school.

RELATIONSHIP FACTORS

The final school factor that surfaced as a compelling issue from our conversations with students was the relationships that were cultivated with teachers and other school personnel. These stories were also often the most heartbreaking because of the striking dichotomy in how students talked about these relationships. On the one hand, students spoke highly of their teachers. For many, their teachers were instrumental in helping them survive. The teachers were their friends. When they faced ostracization from their peers or even just had trouble finding their place, it was often a teacher or other staff member who they said helped them find a place of refuge. That fact made it even harder to hear the stories of teachers who also contributed the most to the racial opportunity cost students experienced, often by saying or doing things that reinforced the white logics that created difficulty for students in the first place. These hardships notwithstanding, it would be impossible to overstate the importance of teachers in the students' experiences. Over and over, students talked about the role of teachers in helping them navigate the challenges they faced. For example, Adriana saw teachers as friends, telling us:

> A lot of my teachers were like my friends. So, I had a really good personal relationship with them outside of school and in school.

Adriana not only had a strong relationship with her teachers in school but was also connected to them outside of school. Like Adriana, Emma also fostered vital relationships—friendships—with her teachers. For her, making friends with people her own age was sometimes challenging as she navigated her school's racialized expectations. As a result, she turned to her teachers for support:

> The deans, the teachers, the security guard, and the lunch ladies. Like, those were my friends.

Emma highlighted an essential point that while teachers, of course, played a central role in students' experiences, so too did other adults in the school. To Emma, the lunch ladies and security guards were just as important to her as the deans and teachers. Therefore, when we think about how we might approach conversations about supporting students in a particular school, we cannot leave these people out because it is likely that they play an important role for students. Emma did not talk about the racial identity of the adults she mentioned, but since it is much more likely for cafeteria workers and security guards to be from racially minoritized backgrounds than teachers, it is quite likely that the interactions that students have with these other adults in the school represent the only opportunities they have to interact with Black and Latinx adults. Further, as the students we spoke to confirmed, those adults are also likely to provide needed encouragement and support to all students, but particularly Black and Latinx students.

Rick also talked about the importance of teachers in his high school experiences. Despite his concerns with how his school responded to the racist incidents that happened while he was there, his teachers retained a fond place in his reflections:

> All the teachers knew me. Like, I was the teacher's pet. I was the one who would bring the teachers gifts and stay after to help them with stuff. I was friends with the principal, even the deans knew me.

As soon as Rick said he was known as the "teacher's pet," we knew what he meant. He was a likable, friendly teen who seemed eager to lend support to anyone around him. We had no trouble imagining him staying after school to help a teacher with a project or bringing them special gifts. However, once we understood the critical role teachers played for Adriana, Emma, Rick, and many of the other students, it was devastating to realize that a respected relationship could be used to cause damage. We already heard from Rick and the ways his teachers and school leaders failed to address the anti-Black racism that permeated the culture of his school. Other students shared additional specific encounters with teachers, even those for whom teachers played a pivotal role. For example, Emma, who talked about the importance of her relationship with teachers, had one encounter with a teacher that she recalled vividly years later:

> I was walking to a class and a teacher just randomly pulled me [aside]. And she's like, "What college are you going to?" To be perfectly honest, I wasn't thinking about going to college. . . . I'm like, "Harvard!" And I thought about it—I was like, "Why can't I? I know I'm in this shithole, but why can't I go to Harvard? Like, why is that beyond me?" She laughed at me. Like, she uproariously laughed at me. And I just remember looking at her, and I'm just like, "You're wrong! How you gonna limit me? No, I want to go to college! What? I'll prove you wrong just like I proved everyone else wrong!"

While we did not know Emma for very long, her determination to achieve whatever she set her mind to came through clearly in our conversation with her. To hear that she decided on the spot that she could go to Harvard was not a surprise to us. However, to hear that her teacher responded by laughing—uproariously—to her was devastating for us to hear. Even many years later, I think about that interaction. While Emma took it as a challenge to "prove her [teacher] wrong," just as she had in so many other situations in her life, I knew that had a teacher said that to me, it likely would have been completely demoralizing. Even the mere suggestion by a peer that I had only gotten into the elite college I first attended because of affirmative action created a spiral of doubts that ultimately led to me leaving that school and spending years making sense of my identity as a "smart Black girl."

Thinking about how the comments of Emma's teacher would have impacted me, I wondered how the students made sense of the comments their teachers made. Rita was the first to share with us what she thought her teachers may have been thinking. Student after student shared stories of encounters with teachers and other school personnel who doubted their ability or questioned whether they belonged. Rita also spoke to us about the low expectations teachers had for racially minoritized students more generally:

> The teachers, some of them just have very low expectations for the students. And so then, it's like this self-fulfilling prophecy. So, when a student doesn't pride themselves—or not even when the student doesn't pride themselves—a student that they're just really struggling. And then, they [the teachers] see that "D" and it's just like, "I knew they wasn't good for nothing. I'm not wasting my time on them." And they just keep going on about they business.

Rita's story reminded me of what Zion had shared earlier about the sailing example his teacher used and his concern that she would interpret his struggles to mean he was not smart. Rita talked about this as a "self-fulfilling prophecy" as she walked us through the ways in which the low expectations teachers had for Black and Latinx students could easily result in their not teaching them as effectively, leading to the students inevitably not doing well in the course. Rick also spoke to this more directly, identifying what was at the heart of the issue of their connections with teachers and why the special relationships students had with them could lead to shattering consequences:

> I think the thing is by being in the position as a student, you think the higher-ups are right in a sense. I mean, like, why am I gonna oppose a teacher who's been here like 15 years? Obviously, he has some legitimacy to what he's saying.

Rick shared a final point here that I connected with. Because the students held teachers in such high regard generally and credited their relationships with them as some of the most important in their lives, what their teachers said *mattered.* This fact only made Rick's analysis of why students may be reticent to question what a teacher said more distressing. If a teacher doubts whether a student can go to Harvard, as Emma's teacher did, or makes them feel like they are not worthy of their time, as Rita suggested, Rick felt that students would be inclined to believe them. "Obviously, [the teacher] has some legitimacy," is what he said. This is why of all the school factors, relationship factors are the most tenuous and the most personal. They were the details that the students recalled with the most emotion and detail, both positively and negatively.

ROC CLOSING THOUGHTS

Across the school factors—climate factors, structural factors, and relationship factors—we saw the ways in which the white logics permeated the students' school environments. This happened through the school climate: the norms and values to which students were expected to aspire, the opportunity to talk openly about race that was cultivated, and the sense of belonging and engagement that was fostered. Structural factors were another place where we saw consequences of these racialized scripts, where seemingly neutral decisions about the classes that students took in fact reinforced and exacerbated racial stratification. Finally, relationship factors highlighted the critical role that teachers—but also other adults like cafeteria workers or security guards—played in students' experiences.

The aspect that connected these issues was their role in making visible the white logics that were imbedded in the students' school environments. Returning to the story that opened this chapter, the principal was working to do just this, hoping—likely with good intentions—to help parents understand the consequences of these racial logics. What was unfortunate about her effort was that she seemed to subscribe to and internalize those white racial logics herself, advancing the idea that wearing head wraps or bonnets could really damage their children's chances at success. In a way, she was right. According to the racialized expectations that saturate our school environments, not aligning with those racialized expectations *could* make it harder for the children to be successful. This idea is not an objective fact, however. It is a social construction. The difference between the two is meteoric. Had she tailored her message to help families understand where these expectations came from, had she explained that they had roots in historical constructions based on white middle-class norms and values, ultimately, she could have helped the students become even more successful. This is a point that Delpit spoke to directly in her work on the culture of power:

> You may have inferred that I believe that because there is a culture of power, everyone should learn the codes to participate in it, and that is how the world should be. Actually, nothing could be further from the truth.... I prefer to be honest with my students. Tell them that their language and cultural style is unique and wonderful but that there is a political power game that is also being played, and if they want to be in on that game there are certain games that they too must play.[5]

Taking a note from Delpit, this principal could have similarly taught her students to use these racial scripts to their favor and been strategic in using them. Perhaps most importantly, they could have learned to do so while remaining connected to and *proud of* their own racial and cultural heritage, not being made to feel that who they were and how they presented themselves was not good enough on its own. At the same time, of course, we can all work to dismantle the racist system that undergirds the whole apparatus. This is the challenge incumbent upon all of us, and the ROC framework can help us in that effort.

ROC Talk: Pay Now or Pay Later? The Hidden Price of Good Schools

Dr. Lolita A. Tabron

A note from Terah Venzant Chambers: Lolita Tabron and I met when I was on the faculty and she was a graduate student at Texas A&M. Over the years, we have remained good friends; she has since moved into a faculty position at a prestigious private university. We have written together on racial opportunity cost and have had extensive conversations about being parents and the importance to us of raising whole, healthy, racially conscious children. In her ROC Talk, Tabron references an aspect of racial opportunity cost that we have presented on at professional conferences but not published about until now: the concept of "pay now or pay later" in the students' experiences. Tabron's perspective on how this concept played out differently for her versus for her husband, and how these experiences impact how she views the road ahead for her children, provides a nuanced and compelling perspective to the ROC framework.

When I think about racial opportunity cost, I think about "pay now or pay later," which takes me back to my K–12 experience. My parents worked hard and sacrificed greatly to make sure my sisters and I could attend good schools. For them, at that time, a good school was well resourced and had everything that typically accompanies a well-funded school—state-of-the-art facilities, well-paid and trained teachers and leaders, easy access to guidance counselors, school psychologists, personal laptops, an expansive curriculum and electives with up-to-date textbooks and equipment like projectors and digital whiteboards, field trips, robust art programs, and gifted and talented programs—basically, the school that every child deserves.

However, what we know from the research is that schools that are well funded are typically predominantly white schools in predominantly white communities. This is largely due to how we fund schools and value assets, particularly Black assets. Many schools still rely heavily on local property taxes, which are based on home values. Higher home values mean higher local property taxes that can be collected to support local schools.

The problem is that often Black neighborhoods, homes, and other assets such as buildings, schools, and land itself are undervalued (until dispossession or gentrification and then these same assets are revalued at a higher market rate). This devaluing of assets through discriminatory property assessments is not just a result of racist perceptions of Black people but a collection of racist housing policies and practices that resulted in the manufacturing of racially segregated neighborhoods. Racist covenant restrictions, policies, and practices have quarantined Black, Brown, and Indigenous communities from the clustering of opportunity and cumulative advantage in white communities. This segregation continues to be perpetuated and fiercely protected today. My family's goal was to build a legacy beyond survival by giving their children access to the best education, even if it came at a literally high cost. However, none of us were aware of the latent effects that would come with this sacrifice.

In fact, our family moved to a small community because my father had read of its high-ranking academic reputation in a national report. This particular high school was the top school in the area. Par for the course, this "good" school was resource-rich, and its outstanding academic reputation increased the value of the neighborhood. This was literally our family's high financial cost of access. However, attending this school had other costs: I did not receive a curriculum or pedagogy that was culturally responsive, and I did not see or experience culturally and linguistically diverse leadership. I sat in classes where my teachers questioned my presence and ability. I experienced a school counselor who did not want to see me graduate with honors (I did, although I could not participate in the ceremony rituals). This counselor continued her racist practice generationally with my sisters by trying to prevent one sister from becoming a part of the National Honor Society and lowering her grade point average (GPA) on a scholarship application that was meant to match her report card. The counselor argued that the school's grading scale was weighted, and that my sister's newly calculated (and lower) GPA was the "more standardized and translatable" GPA for higher education institutions. Yet there is another problem beyond the counselor having crossed out the computer-generated GPA and written in a new one. Universities know which schools operate under a weighted grading system and do their own standardization. So, my sister's GPA was likely lowered in this standardization process by the receiving university a second time! This same counselor also tried to counsel another sister into going into childcare and enrolling in the lowest track of core discipline classes. My parents (particularly my mother) were consistently at the school advocating with us and on our behalf. These are just a few experiences of one family and one counselor. It's not everyone's story, but it is ours and not atypical. What I realize now, reflecting back, was that we were accessing state-of-the-art resources that all children deserve, but also grappling with racism and carrying a burden to prove ourselves and our excellence. And when we did so, which was often, we were tokenized.

Comparatively, my husband attended a predominantly Black school in Gary, Indiana. His school was not well funded or resource-rich, but it was rich in other ways—rich in pride, culture, affirmation, high expectations, and Black excellence. His school was rich in the intangibles, something you would never know, or assume, by looking at traditional metrics.

So, to fast forward: my husband and I attended the same university. He decided to major in computer information systems, despite having very little experience with computers. He quickly realized that he wasn't as prepared as he should have been for his major. He soon learned that the challenging computer programming and coding classes he was struggling in were provided to his white peers in high school. In contrast, the only thing he had learned to do with a computer in high school was how to type. He was forced to dig much deeper in college than his peers to pass his classes; however, it was nothing he couldn't learn and overcome (although he should not have had to overcome this lack of access and poor preparation in the first place). As for me, I started my coursework in stride. However, what I lost in K–12, I'm still fighting to recover to this day as a professor. I refer to the freedom and release from this burden of proof that has accumulated from years of offenses from my K–12 educators and, frankly, what continues today in academic spaces. So, you tell me: Who fared better? I guess you could say that we both did because we're both college-educated professionals. However, I wonder if I would have made different choices or how my path might have been different if I weren't always on the defense or having to prove my value. He paid then. I'm still paying now.

So, for my two daughters, I don't define the quality of a school solely by test scores or the popular data dashboards on real estate websites and applications. Frankly, traditional metrics like test scores, graduation rates, or any other state data measure do not capture what you have to shield and protect your children from or the conversations you must have with teachers, counselors, or principals when your child comes home from school trying to process what they just experienced. When I look at schools, my metrics for quality are different. I look at costs and I look at deposits. I look for knowledge and respect for the community that the school is a part of and their investment in it. I look for their capacity to help nurture my babies' spirits while in their care. Successful schooling to me is that when I send my daughters to school whole, they come back that way, not broken, not questioning. I want them and the school to understand the value of who they are and what they bring to those spaces simply by being themselves.

Terah Venzant Chambers's Take

Reading Lolita's ROC Talk for the first time brought me to tears. First, because she is such a brilliant writer. Second, because she captures with such clarity the central meaning of the ROC framework. I appreciate the broader context she provides in her essay, discussing the legacy of systemic racism and its continued relevance for the context of schooling today. While in this book I highlight what happens at the school level, Tabron offers a timely reminder that schools themselves exist within an environment that influences the resources and opportunities they are able to offer. This does not absolve teachers and school leaders of their responsibility to shift school culture, of course, but it does provide important background.

I was also thrilled that Lolita chose to write about the "pay now or pay later" concept of the ROC work, as this was not something that otherwise would have come up in the book. As Lolita mentions, "pay now or pay later" refers to the seemingly higher ROC for students who attended predominantly white schools, where there were more entrenched racialized norms (the kind of school setting she experienced) as opposed to students who attended schools where racially minoritized students had more freedoms (which is more similar to what her husband experienced). From the ROC participants' stories, we learn that some of these students, like Lolita's husband, may have experienced lower ROC in high school, but when they faced such environments as Northern and Southern College, they were hit with racialized expectations but were less familiar with how to deal with them. In addition, as Lolita discusses because attending schools with larger numbers of racially minoritized students can mean attending schools that are less well resourced, these students may have had to work harder initially to make up lost ground. Thus, students can "pay now" in the sense of higher ROC in white-normed K–12 schools, or "pay later" when they face these environments in college. Sadly, either way, racially minoritized students pay the cost. However, I continue to think about Lolita's husband's being able to make up the academic preparation fairly quickly, whereas she is *still* working to shake off the vestiges of self-doubt that have plagued her from her earliest schooling days.

As Lolita references the differential experiences between her and her husband, I could not help but reflect on similar conversations that I have had with my husband, Glenn Chambers (whose ROC Talk appears later in this book). He and I experienced different K–12 environments similar to what Tabron describes and it has impacted our outlook on the educational opportunities we want for our son. I *do not* think either Tabron or I are saying that our husbands had it "easier" despite attending resource-constrained schools. To suggest that would be to discount the historical realities of urban disinvestment and systemic racism. However, I *do* think we both appreciate the foundation of love and care that they experienced in those environments, which helped buoy them through even the most trying times. That is a significant point to make, especially given the overwhelmingly negative characterizations of Black education that have plagued our society since the times of racially segregated schools (a narrative that scholars like Vanessa Siddle Walker and James Anderson have dedicated their careers to dispel).

As I think about what Lolita's essay means for ROC and the legacy of this framework for the work ahead, I cannot say it better than she did, "When I look at schools, my metrics for quality are different. I look at costs and I look at deposits. I look for knowledge and respect for the community that the school is a part of and their investment in it. I look for their capacity to help nurture my babies' spirits while in their care." Indeed. This is the hope I have for what all Black and Latinx students will experience in school.

CHAPTER 2

Racial Opportunity Costs (ROCs)[1]

> [The University of Chicago Laboratory High School] is a place where jokes about racial and religious identification have been normalized. A place where Black students get their hair gawked at and constantly touched without their permission as if they were animals in a petting zoo. A place where many students of color unfairly feel the need to internalize racist and harmful "jokes" in order to assimilate and survive. A place where we have to sit in classes and have people debate our own existence and identity while sitting demurely as a way to protect ourselves. None of these things are acceptable.

In this excerpt from their open letter to their school, students at the University of Chicago Laboratory High School, known to locals as "Lab," outlined their concerns about the lack of faculty diversity, narrow curriculum, and lackluster response to racist incidents on campus, among other topics.[2] As I read the letter, I knew it could have been written by many of the students I talked to in the ROC study. I could have written it based on my own experiences in school. And yet, too rarely do we hear these stories in the mainstream. Black and Latinx students who are successful in school are often left with the dissonant experiences of feeling isolated and alone while also being lauded for their academic success, held up as a model to which others should aspire. By no means should we diminish their accomplishments. At the same time, pretending as though there is not a *cost* to this success is problematic. The experiences shared by the Lab students in their letter so closely mirrored many of the racial opportunity costs articulated by students I talked to at Northern College and Southern College, who carefully chose their words in order to fit in with expectations and felt like every move they made was being scrutinized. Similarly, the Lab students' expressions of feeling that they needed to "assimilate and survive" mirrored the voices of the students in this project, who attended schools with very narrow racialized performative scripts. These expectations did not lift up the students' cultural histories and traditions; instead, they often disparaged them.

A crucial contribution of the ROC framework is providing nuance and texture to the costs the students incurred. What does it mean to say that academic success comes at a cost? What are those costs? How can we help educators understand the costs that their Black and Latinx students bear? These are the questions I take up in this chapter. From the stories the students shared, I developed three major categories of racial opportunity costs: **psychosocial costs,** which reveal the impact of navigating racialized expectations on students' social and emotional health and well-being; **community costs,** which reflect the difficulty of maintaining a connection with friends, family, and members of the larger racial community while also successfully navigating schools' racialized scripts; and **representation costs,** which detail the responsibility Black and Latinx students felt to be successful on behalf of all members of their racial group, being put "on display" as ambassadors of diversity, and experiencing a heightened sense of scrutiny in classroom and other school spaces. In this chapter, I will address each of these categories in turn.

PSYCHOSOCIAL COSTS

The daily struggle of having to navigate these racialized spaces took a toll on the students in ways that largely went unnoticed by others. Psychosocial costs reflected the aspect of ROC that was the most personal for the students, leaving them to question who they were, whether they belonged, and how to make sense of their identity as high-achieving students given the racialized expectations governing their school culture. I categorized the students' experiences in this area into three themes: questioning their place, feeling isolated and alone, and dealing with racialized identity dissonance.

Questioning their place

Being in spaces where they were the only one or one of few Black and Latinx students was an experience that led many of the participants to doubt their ability to be successful. Adriana, one of the Latina students at Northern College, was used to having her friends around her as a source of support back home in Chicago. Before leaving, she would joke with them about what the experience of going to college would be like. She recounted to us that her friends would say things like, "Man, Adriana, you're going to a school with like all white people. What are you gonna do over there?" At first, she masked her fears by being defensive. She told us, "I came into Northern College kind of like, 'Yeah! Well, I know the answer. What? I can't know it?!'" However, that defensiveness was masking a deeper fear about doing well in college. Elaborating on from where those fears were coming, Adriana told us:

> Coming into Northern College made me more nervous, I think. And not only did I not know what I was getting myself into, but those little comments that we joked about, that didn't help either. Like, it made me so scared to be here. You know? I'm not gonna lie. Every day is a struggle to be out here.

Adriana was nervous that she would not be successful in college. She joked with her friends about what it would be like to be immersed in a predominantly white environment, away from the strong support of her diverse racial community in Chicago. However, beneath the joking was a real concern about whether she fit in that influenced her experience every day and permeated all aspects of her life.

Carla expressed a similar sentiment to Adriana about her doubts about being successful at Northern College, even though her grades were strong:

> I mean, I am still having a hard time giving back to myself sometimes because of what I went through. Sort of, figure out *me*. Last term was so rough for me, I would cry every single night. I would be alone and would try to figure things out. Why am I here? *Like, why am I here?* I mean, I was doing well in classes. I didn't understand how that worked.

Like Adriana, Carla was transitioning to a predominantly white environment for the first time and struggled to find her place at Northern College. When she said she did not "understand how that worked," I took that to mean that she did not understand why she was having such a difficult time in spite of earning high grades in her classes. Despite having concrete evidence that she was doing well, she faced a relentless feeling that she still did not fit in, questioning why she was there. But, of course, it would be confusing. No one talked about these challenges, so how could she know that those feelings were so common? So she kept her struggle to herself, suffering alone.

Had Adriana or Carla known Gregg, he could have shared his insight into the negative implicit messages that often bombard racially minoritized students. According to these messages, they do not fit the racial scripts that permeate their school spaces. Gregg shared with us that at his high school in Texas, people were never shy to share their surprise at his intelligence. "We always got the backhanded compliments. You know, like, 'Oh, you speak so well!' And, you know, 'You write so well! You're really intelligent!' As if it's a surprise." Similarly, Araceli told us that she was seen as an outlier. She shared that "[being a Latina in those advanced classes] was definitely not normal in my high school. It was like, 'Wow!'" Just like Gregg, Araceli noted that people reacted in surprise to see her in those elite spaces. That constant surprise that people expressed, however, was a racial microaggression that Black and Latinx students faced, leading some of them to question whether they belonged in those advanced courses.[3] However, Gregg and Araceli were able to separate themselves from these messages and not internalize them in the same way Adriana and Carla did. They were able to "see" these invisible messages for what they were. It was not Adriana's or Carla's *fault* that they could not. What fueled Adriana and Carla to question their place and what Araceli and Gregg saw in their schools were the white logics that undergird those messages and feelings. Black and Latinx students are not *supposed* to have a place in these advanced classes. It is only natural, though profoundly sad, that some students would internalize those feelings. That internalization added to their racial opportunity cost.

As I will discuss in greater detail in the next chapter, these varying responses to their schools' racial scripts—leading some students to internalize the messages and others to brush them off—are a manifestation of what I call *capacity factors* because they help explain why some students are impacted more than others. These capacity factors also help explain why two students might experience different racial opportunity costs even when they come from similar school environments. However, while a student's capacity to navigate these challenges may vary, we must still remain focused on the reality of the situation they are facing. That is, the problem is with the racialized structures and processes they are navigating; understanding their response to it only enhances our understanding of that broader context so that we can more effectively address it.

Feeling isolated and alone

Another aspect of the psychosocial costs that some students bore was loneliness, an emotion that was tied in to dealing with the literal and figurative exclusion they experienced in their school environment. This resulted in part from racialized tracking that led to their being one of few students of color in their classes, a position some had occupied for years. Similarly, many never quite felt as though they truly fit in with the white students in their classes. Navigating this environment meant that they often felt isolated. Rick, who identified as Black and Puerto Rican, talked about how he did not have a lot of close friends in high school. At the focus group held for students identifying as Latinx at Northern College, Rick shared that he never felt like he had true friends in high school:

> I had a lot of acquaintances. People that you said hello to and that you might eat with once in a while in the cafeteria. But if the topic of politics or maybe race came up . . . [his voice trails off]. Remember, my school is predominantly white, so any discussion I had with them would be automatic disagreement. And they just wouldn't be open to understanding where I was coming from or what I was trying to tell them. So, over time I just said, "Ok, I'm not even gonna talk about that, there's no point because the conversation isn't gonna go anywhere." So just looking at that, I guess I really didn't have any meaningful conversations with anybody.

Not having a place where he could have a real conversation with his peers or teachers created an environment that was incredibly lonely for Rick in high school. There were many times where he needed to have that kind of safe space because of the constant barrage of racist and microaggressive incidents he experienced on a daily basis. However, there were very few other racially minoritized students in his classes. This meant that he was often the "only one" in his classes and thus did not have a community of support. Rick's feeling of isolation occurred as a direct result of his not being in an environment where race was taught about or discussed, which he talked about previously. In Rick's case, his school not having cultivated an open culture created additional tension for Rick and exacerbated the racial opportunity cost he experienced.

However, even when students had other friends of color, they were often still prevented from meaningfully connecting because of a lack of shared experiences: they were usually not in the same classes. As a result, they did not truly understand what each other was battling. Adriana spoke to this issue. Like Rick, she was separated from her same-race friends, though for her it was due to racialized tracking and her participation in elite programs outside of her school. Unlike Rick, there were actually a fair number of racially minoritized students in her school overall. She tried to maintain a connection with her friends, but the lack of common experiences took a toll. She told us, "A lot of my friends would always be like, 'Where are you going now? Oh. Oh, you're going to [a third-party mentoring program for gifted students]? Okay. Go.'" Her friends were supportive of her efforts and they wanted her to be successful.

That the students we spoke with received positive affirmations from members of their racial community for their achievements was not unusual. However, the separation nonetheless strained these friendships and the students reported feeling isolated and alone as a result. Connecting the isolation and loneliness Adriana felt to the school factors shared in the previous chapter, it is clear that the structural factors—here, racialized tracking—played a significant role in her feelings of isolation and loneliness. In this way, the figurative distancing Adriana felt was due at least in part to the physical distancing she experienced due to racially stratified classes in her school.

Racialized Identity Dissonance

Simply exploring the students' sense of doubt about their ability to be successful in their white-normed environments as well as the profound feelings of loneliness and isolation they felt should already make clear that navigating their identities as Black and Latinx students in these racialized spaces was a significant challenge for them. As a result, a third category of the psychosocial costs related to the toll it took on the students to navigate these elite academic spaces when those spaces refused to make space for their racial identity. This is tricky territory to navigate, though, and so a bit of explanation is needed before sharing the students' stories.

Existing research did not offer a term that quite expressed what the students discussed. I had previously talked about this ROC as the students "struggling with racial identity"[4] to highlight the need for them to conform to the white logics that ruled the performative expectations in their classrooms. This burden sometimes caused them to question who they were and whether they were smart enough or the "right" kind of person to inhabit that space, as was expressed from the stories shared by Carla and Adriana at the beginning of this section. However, I have never been happy with the connotation that the students themselves were struggling, or that the struggle was something they manifested. Employing the language that way seemed to inadvertently contribute to deficit thinking by situating the problem as originating within the student. This was obviously not my intention, so I continued to search for a term that more effectively called attention to the environment's role in manifesting this tension.

In looking for a way to better capture the students' experience, I considered the term *racial dissonance*, but soon learned that this was an existing term used in psychology.[5] In her research, Dr. Keisha Bentley-Edwards defined racial dissonance:

> [S]ome Blacks may have a strong sense of racial dissonance toward other Blacks that is represented by ambivalence and antagonism. Racial dissonance is represented by a distinct disconnect between a person and his or her racial community that includes disdain or discomfort in Black racial contexts, and a lack of empathy for impoverished Blacks. Although internalized oppression may serve as a key influence on racial dissonance, racial self-hatred cannot be assumed. A person high in racial dissonance may have a positive self-appraisal as a Black person, but he or she will simultaneously stereotype and accept societal views of other Blacks.

She explained that racial dissonance could be contrasted with racial cohesion, which reflected a high degree of connectedness with members of the same racial group. I was pleased to see that this was an issue that other scholars were discussing and found that while these terms were close to what the students I talked to experienced, neither of them, racial cohesion nor racial dissonance, quite matched what I was looking for to explain the patterns I saw in the students' experiences. Thus, I offered the term *racialized identity dissonance* as a way to capture the struggle some students had in trying to make sense of what it meant to be a Black and Latinx student in these school spaces imbued with white logics. I saw this concept as different from racial dissonance for a few reasons.

First, the students did not necessarily have disdain for their same-race peers. They were trying to figure out *what* they felt in an environment that gave them little support to understand what was happening. They did experience dissonance, so that part felt right. However, the dissonance they experienced resulted from having to make sense of what it meant for them to be in contexts where there were no or very few other Black and Latinx students. It would be fair to suggest that some of these students had internalized a negative impression of other racially minoritized students; however, I maintained that this orientation resulted from the absence of other students who looked like them and their internalization of the "backhanded compliments" that Gregg discussed earlier in this chapter that result from the school's white logics. The schools often reinforced these feelings, lauding students—even in a well-meaning way—for how "special" they were for their academic accomplishments. However, this only fueled the students' confusion because it indicated that their accomplishments were somehow unusual.

Elsie shared a story that helped characterize this tension, what I now call *racialized identity dissonance.* She was a Northern College student who identified as African American/Eritrean. She attended a fairly diverse high school in in a large city in the South. Nonetheless, she talked about the struggles she experienced making sense of her identity as a Black girl:

> In elementary school and middle school, I was called "Oreo": Black on the outside, white on the inside. I was kind of. . . . Like, I wasn't acting Black enough. But, I mean, what *is* acting "Black enough," or how *do* you act in a certain way, is my question. I don't really care as much because I didn't really have any Black friends [before I got to] college. I always had either Asian or white friends or African friends, not like African American friends. So, it was extremely different. I think that that kind of peer pressure was extremely uncomfortable. . . . All of the African American students [at my high school] kind of associated with each other. So, even though they were smart, they still associated with individuals who, you know, "did things" or were a part of the crew and whatnot. . . . So, at times, I did feel like I am betraying my race, like I'm either thinking I'm too good to be with them but I also realized that it is not that.

There is so much to unpack from Elsie's story. She talked about the struggle she faced being seen as an "oreo" by other students of color. She did not understand why her peers were calling her that, nor did she understand why she was not seen as "Black enough." Certainly, having parents who had emigrated from East Africa created a different situation for her from other Black students. She was negotiating that additional layer of being the daughter of immigrant parents who did not understand the U.S. racial dynamics she was encountering in school.

However, Elsie also provided perspective into what was happening with other Black students in her school who were strongly connected with each other even "though they were smart," as she said. Elsie illustrated the point I made above that "racial dissonance" alone does not entirely capture her experience. In some ways, she seemed to meet the definition of expressing disdain for Black students by saying she felt like she might have been "too good" to be associated with them and that most of her friends were white, Asian, or African. However, she also pushed back against that idea. She did not have the words to make sense of it at the time, but she had an innate understanding that there was a different answer just out of her grasp. As she said, "I realized that it is not that," that she was not better than other Black students in her school. By her own assessment, those Black students were smart. The situation was hard for her to explain.

Reading her words, we can see her pushing back against the racialized expectations she had internalized about African American students at that earlier time in her life. Even in her diverse high school, racialized messages about who was smart or what it took to be successful were still pervasive. Elsie was able to separate from that by associating with non-African American students, but she conveyed her discomfort with the idea that she had to do that, especially with the perspective she had gained by being in college and being around more African American students. In her mind, her separating from them led her to be successful. However, when she said the words out loud, she understood that explanation did not make sense.

Elsie made the point that she was not friends with African American students so much in high school, but that this changed in college. Interestingly, Elsie was closely aligned with African American students at Northern College, and this was an important part of her identity when we talked with her. This is an important point to consider: although her seeming disdain for other African American students may have been perceived to reflect "racial dissonance," she explained that she never felt comfortable with those feelings. Further, she turned away from those feelings completely once she was at Northern College, where she could spend meaningful time with other Black students. She was also given the tools in classes and other extracurricular clubs with which to make sense of her experiences and talk about race more openly. As a result of this change in perspective and environment, she struggled in our interview to convey her thinking from back in high school. Thus, it was not that she had disdain for African American students, but rather that she was ill prepared by her teachers and school leaders to make sense of the racialized dynamics of her school environment.

Thus, another important aspect of racialized identity dissonance was that it encompassed the reality that these students' navigation of racial identity came as a result of interacting with the white logics present in their spaces. These psychological constructs were obviously rooted in an intrapersonal analysis. However, I needed a term that would point to this process as interactive with the larger school environment. I made a similar distinction in chapter 1, where I discussed the term *racialization* and how it reflects this institutional perspective. Our focus should be on the system, not just the individuals that comprise it. In a similar way, then, I used the term *racialized identity dissonance* to reflect the struggle some students had in trying to make sense of their identity as Black and Latinx in light of these larger institutionalized racial dynamics. Having established the foundation for the concept of racialized identity dissonance, hearing stories from other students about their experiences with it may provide additional clarity.

Carla addressed the racialized identity dissonance she experienced as a result of her peers and others around her seeing her as "white" for the way she spoke. Navigating the ways people spoke in different contexts began to weigh on her, though, as she expressed to us in her interview:

> It is so hard because sometimes I shut myself from that, from my racial identity, and just focus on academics. And the way I talk at home is of course different from the way I talk in the classroom. [For] white students, the way they talk at home is the way they talk in the classrooms. So, having to separate that, a part that is me, you know what I mean? I don't know the dictionary, but it is like a whole new language. . . . I can relate to that. I mean, it hurts when people tell me it is white.

The challenge Carla faced navigating how she spoke in one context to the next was not something her white peers needed to navigate. Rather, for her it was like needing to learn "a whole new language" that was different from the language she used at home. On top of that challenge, she was labeled as white because of the way she talked. This was hard for her to make sense of, too, because she could "relate to" that language but struggled to understand what it meant to be seen as white because of it. None of this is about Carla, specifically. She did not do anything wrong. Rather, the issue was the racial logics present in her school and the additional challenges that navigating them created for her.

This idea of academic success or making it into elite educational spaces while being seen as "white" came up in other interviews as students grappled with how to express what I saw as their recognition of the white logics that permeated their school culture (even if they did not use that language). For example, Emma talked about how even though she felt strong in her racial identity, the questions others asked still took a toll on her:

> And so, I'm doing well. And then all of a sudden, I lose my identity, and I become white. And I'm just like, "Shit!" You know? How do you do that? Why can't it just be, "You sound smart"? And as far as being able to hold your racial identity, you lose it. As much as you try to keep it, as much as people do try to hold onto it, like you lose it in the social realm.

When Emma said, "I become white," she did not mean that she was seen as a white student or that she wanted to be white. Rather, she was grappling with the fact that there were no other options for her in this space. In her school, the identities of "Latina" and "smart" did not go together. As a result, it was a continuous battle for her to maintain her academic success *and* have her identity be validated. In order to be seen as smart, she was also seen either as white or wanting to be white *despite* her personal feelings or identity.

While Emma and some of the students felt strongly about expressing their racial identity despite the challenges it created for them at school, other students did not feel that they could express their racial identity at all. Ice seemed to experience the greatest degree of racialized identity dissonance of all of the students with whom we talked. He received mixed messages at school, from his peers, and from his family. As a result, he had a difficult time making sense of his identity. Like Emma, he also likened the experience to being (seen as) white. Talking about his interactions with others, Ice said:

> They'll never even say "assimilation" like to just sum it up. They'll just be like, "Why you talk like you white?" You hear that a lot. Or, "You think you smart?" But they say it as if it's negative. I mean, "Why you talk like you white?" That can be actually quite negative 'cause it means that you talk like that because you've gone on to try to educate yourself. But along the way, you're talking like someone who, like, uh, you're, you are kinda assimilating into that culture, which I don't. I don't feel like you should have to do. You, you shouldn't, you shouldn't have to do. Um, personally. You, you kinda, I mean, you, yeah, you kinda do. Maybe. . . .

Ice struggled to clearly convey his thoughts here because it was a complicated circumstance to explain. However, even as his sentences started and stopped and he tried over and over to articulate his point, it was actually quite clear. He did not feel like he *should* have to assimilate into his school's white-normed culture in order to be successful. At the same time, he still felt it was (regrettably) necessary to do so in order to be successful in his school. This tension he described perfectly encapsulated the racialized identity dissonance that some students experienced and why I labeled this a racial opportunity cost.

Carla, Ice, and Emma were not the only students who dealt with being accused of "acting white" because they took advanced classes. Melody, an African American student at Southern, also spoke to this experience, telling us:

> [People make] the assumption, "Oh, you're smart, so you act white." Some people can either choose to stop, like, paying attention in class and doing their work so they can fit in, or they just stop hanging out with Black people.

Melody was better able to separate herself from these accusations so that she did not take it personally when people made these assumptions about her. But she saw that it was more difficult for other students, who may have felt that they needed to either "stop paying attention in class" in order to maintain their connection to other students of color, or "stop hanging out with Black people" if they wanted to stay in those more advanced classes. For most Black students in her school, it was not easy to maintain a connection with other Black students *and* do well in class. These two positions should not be at such odds with one another. And yet student after student talked about the tension they felt being smart *and* Black and Latinx.

The students' discussions about being seen as white for striving to achieve academic success in their schools despite the prevailing messages that Black and Latinx students did not belong in those elite academic spaces is reminiscent of a body of scholarship originating with Fordham and Ogbu and their "acting white" phenomenon.[6] However, while there are similarities, I want to be clear that my analysis brings me to a substantially different conclusion from Fordham and Ogbu's. According to their research findings, the collective identity and fictive kinship tradition of Black culture are formed in opposition to white culture. Thus, they maintain, activities that are aligned with white culture, like academic achievement, are rejected by Black students out of a fear of being seen as "acting white." There are aspects of this work that may seem to resonate with what the students discussed in the excerpts shared above about being seen as being or acting white as a result of their pursuit of academic success. However, there are two important departures in my analysis from Fordham and Ogbu's work.

The first departure is the way their assertions fall into the trap of deficit thinking, blaming the students for their "ambivalence" toward academic achievement.[7] As I have tried to argue with the concept of racialized identity dissonance and with the ROC work more generally, the struggle the students experienced did not originate internally. Rather, the dissonance they experienced stemmed from the racialized environments they navigated. The second departure from Fordham and Ogbu's work on acting white is their assertion of the association of academic achievement with white culture as a specific feature of Black culture. As I have demonstrated in this chapter and reviewed as part of the literature in chapter 1, the idea that schools are sites of the creation and perpetuation of white logics is an established idea across a vast array of scholarship. Suggesting that Black people have somehow made up that idea is not only misleading, but is a perverse manifestation of deficit thinking in service of those same white logics.

In this section, the students demonstrated the emotional toll of navigating the racialized expectations in their schools and of making sense of what it meant for them to exist in defiance of those expectations. They questioned whether they belonged in these elite spaces, felt lonely and isolated from others, and experienced racialized identity dissonance as a result of trying to make sense of their outlier status as smart *and* Black and Latinx students. Each of these were aspects of the psychosocial costs of the ROC framework.

COMMUNITY COSTS

Another powerful category of racial opportunity cost that emerged from the students' stories was a feeling of being disconnected from peers, family, and their larger racial community. Pursuing academic success meant performing in alignment with the racialized expectations present in their schools. As discussed in the literature review and previously in this chapter, those expectations sometimes conflicted with those of their racial community. Navigating these different expectations often created strain on the students' close relationships because it could seem like the students were *rejecting* their peers and family. Even as students received encouragement from those who were closest to them, the path they took nonetheless left many feeling a sense of distance from those with whom they were closest.

Losing a connection to African American and Latinx friends

This theme is likely not surprising to see because a sense of distancing from friends can be inferred from many of the stories students have shared so far in this chapter. However, the students also spoke to this issue directly, and I want to share just one example from a particularly poignant story. When we asked Elsie to explain why Black students whom she said were smart enough to take the high-track classes she was enrolled in did not, she pointed to the potential loss of friendships they feared might happen:

> I think that individuals don't do it because their friends don't do it. I think a lot of it has to do with a lot of that. Everything I did in high school was pretty much associated with what my friends did. So, it really depends on who you tend to hang out with. Would you risk losing that group or the support system that you believe may *possibly* [make you] successful? Because you never know what may happen to you.

Elsie pointed out that there were risks involved in taking advanced classes; potentially damaging one's relationship with friends was a significant one. In a student's calculation, why give up that support system for the *possibility* that it will help you become successful later? And even if you believe that taking those classes might increase your chance for success, is it worth giving up a connection with the people about whom you care the most to do it? This was not an issue for Elsie because most of her friends, who at this stage in her life were primarily white, Asian, and African, were in her classes. But she understood that if her friends had not taken those advanced classes, it would have been difficult for her to enroll in them alone. This perspective provided important context to the loneliness and isolation other students discussed. Rick's story from the previous section comes to mind, where he talked about only having acquaintances, not true friends, in his classes. He bore the cost of not having a support system with him every day. Elsie bolstered this point by suggesting that some students might see that as such a high price that they did not even want to risk the possibility of becoming disconnected from their friends, especially since taking advanced classes was not a sure shot to success, either. The safer choice might be to stay in the less challenging classes surrounded by a reassuring network of friends.

Losing a connection to African American and Latinx family

While feeling separated from friends was certainly difficult for many students, the distancing from family they experienced took an even deeper toll. Though their families were often encouraging of their pursuit of academic achievement, the students' navigation of white-normed expectations nonetheless fostered a feeling of distance or disconnection. While many families were supportive, there were others who did not understand the difficulty of what the students were facing. Ice shared that one member of his family seemed to take his choice personally, expressing that he was trying to be better than from where he came. As he explained:

> One of [my aunts] asked me, "Could you go to the gas station?" They're from the South. So, they have like very strong accents, very country-soundin' accents. But, I responded in the way that I'm talking now. And she like snarls her lip. And she's like, "Errr!"

In our conversation with him, Ice said that while some students were able to code-switch—falling into speech patterns that were seen as "appropriate" to the particular setting they were in—he himself had lost the ability. He spoke "properly" wherever he went, which led to the encounter he described above, where his aunt responded to his speech patterns with disdain.

The topic of negotiating relationships with family also came up at the African American focus group at Northern College. Carla talked about the sadness she felt when her family did not share her enthusiasm for what she learned at school. This made it difficult to find ways to remain connected with them. As she explained:

> It's so hard [to keep a connection to family] when I have school. . . . I'll start talking. And then, somebody in my family would be like, "Well, stop talking," or "I don't want to hear that." But that kind of hurts because I really care about things. But, I don't want to sit there and be the girl that talks about what she learned at school all day. . . . Because school is something that I love, having to hold back just so that I don't make other people feel uncomfortable—especially the people that I love—[is hard].

As soon as Carla finished talking, Alexa jumped into the conversation to make the following point:

> And to add on to what Carla is saying—'cause I understand completely. It just feels like your family is moving in this circle. . . . And then, you're growing, and you're outside of the circle. And as you go higher in education, you're moving further away from the circle that's going in this cycle. And so, once you [go] back [home], it's like . . . everything remains the same. I guess it *seems* like everything is the same. But you just don't fit in that circle anymore.

Alexa picked up on the disconnection from family that Carla expressed and they both shared how hard it was to maintain a connection with family when separated from them literally, figuratively, or both. In this particular situation, Alexa was talking about being separated by distance, having gone to college in a different state; however, the separation from family that Carla talked about was more figurative. In her individual interview with us, Alexa had expanded on her thoughts about not feeling understood by her family:

> If you come from a neighborhood where the demographics or the economic status or whatever is like lower or middle class, and most of your friends are from that area, when you choose those AP classes there becomes a disconnect between you and your friends. Like, I see it every time I go home. . . . I don't know my family members. Sometimes being around them is just hard because they don't understand me. And I no longer understand them. [We ask her how that impacted her.] Kids, they just get tossed out of their community, or the community that they identify with most. And then they end up having to find a new one with people who probably won't look anything like them.

Alexa elaborated on how difficult it was for her to stay connected with her family. To her, being ostracized from one's family and being forced to foster a sense of community with people who do not share the same racial identity was difficult to manage. For too many students we talked with, attending college in these elite spaces and following the path that took them there moved them further away from their families. As Carla said earlier in the chapter, her white peers were able to speak in the same way at home and at school: they did not have to juggle these consequence or suffer the same feelings of disconnection. Their environments were more aligned.

I think it might be easy to place blame on the families in this situation, to judge Ice's aunt for the way she responded to his proper speech, for example, or to criticize Alexa or Carla's families for not understanding what they were going through. The point is not to cast blame on the families, but rather to understand what the cost is to the students when they have to navigate this challenging terrain. I also want to underscore the point that that the implications of the ROCs that students experience extended beyond themselves to their families and larger community. To that point, since we did not speak with the families directly, we cannot fully understand what this felt like from their perspective. However, we can speculate about it. What does it mean when your child or nephew starts to speak, act, or dress differently or to suddenly start hanging out with the white students in their classes? I imagine it might feel like rejection. It is just not as simple as a family needing to be more accepting or open minded. Again, this would indicate that the blame lies with the families. Instead, we should be asking why schools put students in situations of speaking, dressing, and/or or behaving in ways that separate them from their families. We also need to understand the cost to students when mirroring their school's expectations moves them further from their family and they are left to make sense of that disconnection. With all that said, I do want to reiterate the point that most of the students shared that their families were, overall, incredibly supportive of them. In fact, that support is what helped many of them navigate these challenges in the first place. This is why family is identified as an important capacity or protective factor, which I discuss further in chapter 4.

Losing a connection to the larger African American and Latinx community

The final aspect of ROC related to community costs was the lost connection to the students' larger racial community. Although this ROC was perhaps the least personal, especially compared to the difficulty of negotiating relationships with family and friends, it was possibly the most impactful overall. One important theme that emerged from many of the students' stories, particularly those who had grown up in urban areas, was the amazing support they received from their community. I referenced this fact several times earlier in this chapter both because it was a common theme but also because it offers a counternarrative to prevailing negative stereotypes about these communities. Across many of the students' interviews, they discussed the broad support received from what might be seen as unexpected sources. I want to establish this point first to highlight that these were critical aspects of the students' community. Despite negative stereotypes about their racial community, there was a lot of good that came from these connections. For example, Moe talked about how other Black folx in his neighborhood would encourage him to continue on his path of doing well in school:

> [Someone] would like come over in some low rider or whatnot, not really scaring me that much but making me wonder what they are doing. And then saying, "Good job!" Or like, not necessarily, "Thank you," but "Way to show people that we are not just trash."

Moe received encouragement from the people in his neighborhood. He may not have known them personally, but they knew who he was either from his siblings or other connections. It was clear that they were discussing his success in school positively. In that sense, his reputation preceded him. Similarly, Carla shared that in her school, students who may have been engaged in illegal activities were nonetheless supportive of her success:

> But even guys like the drug dealers in my high school, who are hardcore, would be like, "You're really cool, you go places." That hurt because it's like saying you are unique, go ahead, just go ahead. I am like, "Why can't you come with me with me?" I could not understand that. I love those guys but they are so misunderstood. They are special. Now, it is hard because, I mean, I would motivate who I could. I would always do my best.

While many students in the project noted their disconnection from members of their racial community, Carla questioned why that disconnection needed to happen in the first place. She did not understand why she should have to leave the community of supporters—as unlikely as some of them may have been—as she continued to "go places." Further, she worried that leaving them would also mean she would not be there to motivate them and remind them that "they are special." While her words are sweet, the underlying point highlights a vital question: Who would tell these students that they care about them and that they are special when Carla left?

While the stories Moe and Carla shared established the idea that members of the broader racial community could serve as an important source of support for the students, it was Zion who talked about the impact that being removed from that community would have. Speaking to what it meant to him to see older kids from his neighborhood go off to college, get jobs, and never come back home, Zion said:

> You can lose connection with the Black community as a whole. And if you get your "A" and you go on to college and all this kinda stuff, if you like lose that connection, especially early on, then you can't—it's really hard to get it back. Especially once you're like in college and you've already lost it in high school. . . . Then, once you graduate high school, you gettin' this good career or whatever, I don't think you're gonna try and help out other students like you. Or, even go back and try and say, "Oh, well, it's good to do this. . . ." You lose a lot. And then, the whole community as a whole loses a lot 'cause they lose another role model. . . . You can't really have a role model that doesn't care about you.

When he was younger, Zion saw older kids go to college and not return. Because of this experience, he was keenly attentive to the issue and was committed to returning back home to serve as a role model for younger kids from his neighborhood. There were two important ways to interpret Zion's quote. The first was that he spoke to the loss the entire racial community experienced when young people went off to college and pursued "good careers" but never came back. What message did that send to those who were younger? That you could achieve these great things but it means giving up everything you've ever known? The second related point—and Elsie made a similar point in the story I shared earlier in the chapter—was that it gave another layer of insight into the choices other "smart" Black and Latinx students made who also had the capacity to do well in school. But why? If going to college and getting a good job ultimately meant being separated from family and friends and everything you care about, why do it? If choosing to pursue academic success literally costs everything you care about, if we have made it so impossible for students to remain connected to where they come from, how can we expect them to make that choice? This point is perhaps the most poignant implication of community costs: the collective, cumulative cost incurred by the broader racial community resulting from the white logics that permeate schools and other societal spaces.[8]

REPRESENTATION COSTS

As outlined previously in this chapter, being a high-achieving Black or Latinx student came with a host of ROCs—from feeling isolated and lonely in their white-normed school spaces to feeling disconnected from friends and family. The realities of these costs make the last category of ROC that much more ironic. Even as they were struggling to find their place in these spaces, they were often laden with the additional burden of being the ambassadors of diversity, of being held up as a model of what other students of color should hope to achieve. These representations costs are expressed in three different ways in this section: representing for all African American and Latinx students, being the poster child for diversity, and dealing with the constant state of being on display.

Representing for all African American and Latinx students

A common aspect of the representation costs that emerged from our analysis of the stories the students shared with us was the sense of collective responsibility they felt to do well, to show that racially minoritized students were capable of being successful in advanced classes and deserved their placements in them. Melody made her feeling on this issue quite plain in her interview, telling us:

> Sometimes I felt like I was having to represent for the Black students. And, I mean, it made me proud, though. At graduation when I got certain awards, [my friends] were like, "Oh, Melody, you represent for us." And that made me happy. But I generally was the only one.

There were only a small number of Black students in her religious private school to begin with, most of whom were not as successful as Melody in navigating the racialized expectations in school. As a result, she felt an additional pressure to do well herself on their behalf. Melody expressed that she was proud to represent other Black students. And that is wonderful. Many students talked positively about that pressure—but it was pressure, nonetheless. Micayla made a similar point in her individual interview, feeling a similar responsibility to Melody to show that Black students could do well in advanced classes:

> When you are a minority, it's like you are just not representing yourself. You are representing your entire race whenever you step into a classroom. I think there's more of a responsibility that you end up taking on when you do enter that high-achieving [space]. . . . Instead of being, you know, the really smart Black person with the whole group of Black people, you're like the smart [Black] person with the whole group of high-achieving white students.

Micayla felt that she had an additional burden to bear as one of the few Black students in the advanced classes. She felt that her racial identity was emblazoned on her head every time she entered a classroom space, that it was not just Micayla she was doing well for, but all Black students.

Araceli shared a similar sentiment. In response to her sharing a story about being one of the only Latinas in her school taking advanced-track classes, we asked if she ever felt pressure to speak or dress in a particular way. She told us, "I don't care. You know, for me, it was like I was showing them that Hispanic students could also achieve in any kinda community. So, for me, it was like, 'No. We can do this, too.' You know?" Araceli took it as a challenge to push back against the prevailing norms that Latinx students were not expected to achieve much.

An additional irony was that in many schools, students carried the responsibility of demonstrating that Black and Latinx students could be successful, while some teachers used that success to create or exacerbate tensions between students. Emma spoke to this when she shared how one teacher would broadcast her success to other students, straining those already tenuous relationships even further:

> I remember getting my test scores, getting the test back and hurrying and like hiding them because getting good test scores was bad and then later finding out that my teachers were over there saying things like, "Oh, yeah, Emma got this and this grade. Oh, you should be more like Emma." I'm out here trying to be friends with people, and they are over there like making that impossible for me.

Perhaps her teachers thought that sharing Emma's success would be encouraging to other racially minoritized students. However, they did not understand the dynamics of the situation that the students were already struggling to navigate. Thus, for a teacher to interject and say that other students should aspire to be "more like Emma" actually exacerbated those tensions and was an additional ROC related to representing for other students of color.

Being the poster child for diversity

If the students felt a responsibility to represent for other Black and Latinx students, many of the schools did not waste a moment in capitalizing on those feelings. Many schools were almost too eager to highlight the students' elite status, inviting them to appear in photos, meet with school visitors, and otherwise represent the school's (often otherwise nonexistent) commitment to diversity. Or to benefit from the students' skills when it was convenient, like with Araceli, who told us that she was sometimes called upon to provide (free) Spanish-to-English translation when it was needed. Rick spoke to this issue of being an ambassador of diversity in his interview:

> [I] got picked for a lot of things . . . for high school to represent, you know, sit in on somebody speaking. Or like, "Go eat lunch with this person who's like a visiting speaker. Go eat dinner with them to represent the school and have discussions."

There were very few Black or Latinx students at Rick's school, which, as discussed earlier in this chapter, contributed to his feelings of isolation and loneliness. However, that isolation did not stop the school from expecting him to entertain outsiders. On top of his school work, extracurricular activities, and other responsibilities, he was expected to make room for these kinds of diversity ambassador opportunities whenever they were presented to him. Emma also spoke to this pressure in her interview, expressing that, ideally, she would have liked to just focus on her schoolwork. However, her school wanted more from her:

> You can't just be a student, you have to be diversity personified . . . and that really upset me because all I wanted to do was be a student, because that's hard enough.

Emma felt this expectation to be "diversity personified" was an additional burden that, like Rick, she was expected to carry. Rather than just doing well in courses, which was difficult in itself given the commitments she had at school and at home, she was also expected to take on these additional obligations. Across the student interviews, we noted that many students expressed similar expectations to take on these roles as diversity ambassadors in their school.

Being on display

The first two representation factor categories I discussed here had to do with students feeling responsible for proving that students of color were capable of doing well in advanced classes or for demonstrating the school's commitment to diversity. The third category had to do with the toll that resulted from actually being in those spaces every day. The cost of this academic pressure is reflected in the previous discussion. Not reflected yet is the students' feeling that they were always on display in these classes. They were perceived not to belong there. Their classmates and teachers seemed always to be looking for evidence to prove that point. Every movement, every word, was scrutinized, as Micayla discussed:

> I'll never forget one time. I dropped something, and I said, "It ain't broke." And they kept asking me, "Is it broken?" And I'd be like, "It ain't." I said, "It ain't broke," like three or four times, and I didn't understand why they kept asking me And they were all laughing. They were laughing because I said, "It ain't broke." You know, it's stuff like that. And so, I was just kinda like, "Really now? Is it that hilarious?"

In this example, Micayla was speaking in African American Vernacular English, saying "it ain't broke" when she saw that her pencil was still intact. However, her saying "it ain't broke" instead of the expected "it isn't broken" opened her up to ridicule from her white peers. Micayla went on to talk about how because of incidents like this, she was always very careful about how she presented herself in the spaces she entered, particularly in how she spoke.

Jessica, another Southern College Black student, told us that her way of dealing with this increased scrutiny was to "tone herself down" when she was in class with white students:

> Since it was all white people, I know they joke. Obviously, I'm not that ghetto. But I was the most ghetto one in Honors. And so, I mean, I know. And I'm not. I guess 'cause that means everyone else was less toned down.

Seeing her struggle to explain what she meant, I asked a clarifying question, "What do you mean by 'less toned down'? Like, do you feel that you were different in those classes from the way you normally were in real life?" To this she responded:

> I mean, I guess. 'Cause the people I was around. . . . Like, if I was around just the Black people, I would probably act differently with them. 'Cause, I didn't really . . . um . . . joke around with white people as much or use the same jokes. So, I guess you do like change and adapt.

From talking with many students about this issue, I understood Jessica's discomfort with talking about her adaptations. It was hard to talk about changing her behavior to better fit in because she may have been a bit embarrassed or uncomfortable to admit that these were decisions she made or even just thought about. When we talked to Jessica, she had not yet participated in the focus group with other students. This was true for all of the students because we purposefully tried to hold the individual interviews with students before hosting the focus group. These were topics many of the students had never talked about, and they felt all kinds of emotions about what they did and why (like Elsie, who struggled to explain the strained relationship she had with African American students discussed at the beginning of this chapter). In Jessica's case, she found it difficult to talk about the choices she made. Many of the students struggled with the tension between what they *wanted* to do or say and how they *actually* behaved or talked in their predominantly white classes. But they did not realize how challenging the situation was that they were dealing with, nor that there were so many other students who felt the same way.

Zion relayed a similar perspective to Jessica's and Micayla's in that he was careful about what he presented to his white peers. At home with his family, he could be his true, authentic self. But he was careful about being so free at school, especially with his music choices:

> The music I play, I try and sensor it 'cause I don't want the N-word or things like that being played with my door open. Or people hearing it. Especially the white students hearing it and then thinking, "Oh, if he's listening to it and if he's saying it, then it's okay for me to say."

Zion's sense of increased scrutiny was most salient in terms of how he presented himself and the music he listened to while in his dorm room. He was aware that his white peers might interpret his listening to music with explicit lyrics as license to use those words themselves. He did not want them to use their relationship with him as permission to engage in inappropriate or racist behaviors—and he felt that was a responsibility he shouldered.

Students had many strategies for coping with being in these white-normed spaces. Micayla learned to choose her words carefully. Jessica presented a "toned down" version of her usual dynamic personality. Zion was thoughtful about the music he listened to and when. However, Rita took another path, deflecting attention away from her racial identity by using humor. As she said:

> A lot of times, when I talked to [people from] other cultures, it was just because I was the comedian in the high school. So, I would be cracking jokes and stuff. "Rita, you're so funny!" [said in a high, sing-song voice . . . . So, that was the way that I got across to [people from] other cultures. And, they'd be like, "Rita is so funny. She just says whatever is on her mind and she doesn't care." But no. I never dressed like them and never talked like them. And none of my friends did, either. It was just, like, who we are.

It was interesting that Rita was adamant about choosing not to dress or talk like the white students in her classes but still felt that some kind of adaptation was necessary. She turned to humor to cope with the hyper-scrutiny she experienced in her classes. They may have gone about it in different ways, but nearly all of the students expressed that they made some kind of accommodation to make their experiences in school more bearable.

In this chapter, the stories the students shared helped clarify the complex nature of the school environments they navigated. At this developmental stage, friendships with peers are incredibly significant. Yet, most of these students were separated from this support system as a result of racialized tracking. This separation led to a variety of psychosocial costs that impaired their social and emotional health and well-being. They were also left to deal with a host of community costs because even as they were reeling from feelings of loneliness and isolation, they faced the additional burden of navigating tenuous relationships with friends, family, and the larger racial community who did not always understand what they were going through. Finally, even as they battled to overcome these challenges, the students were hit with the additional burden of representing for all students of color while also experiencing a sense of hyper-scrutiny, feelings that adults in the school often exacerbated.

These stories paint a picture of a population of students in need of critical attention. The very skills that allowed them to be successful in such hostile spaces were the same ones that might make what they were doing look easy and lead to assumptions that they are doing well. "Smile and meet with the visiting scholars!" "Aren't these students so amazing?" All the while, the students were often navigating overwhelming feelings of disconnection and loneliness and had no one to talk to about them.

ROC CLOSING THOUGHTS

I want to return briefly to the open letter from the Chicago Lab students that I used to begin this chapter. I was inspired by these young Chicagoans, who took a stand to demand better for themselves and future racially minoritized Chicago Lab students. Whether they knew it when they wrote the letter, the experiences they shared were common to so many high-achieving students of color in schools across the country. They closed their letter with a critical request:

> We implore that this letter is understood as one piece of work, as we do not have the option to leave our race at the door; it is a part of our existence and should not just be a topic to discuss. . . . We do not intend that this letter have all the immediate solutions to the problems presented; we want this to be a first step in truly making a difference.

The students were right. Race was not something that they could leave at the door. Facing that reality must be the foundation of whatever comes next. However, I disagree with the students on one thing. While students must be a part of any solution to these challenges, it is *our* job as educators to recognize the problems and take on the responsibility of addressing them. We have not fully understood or been appropriately attentive to the challenges these students navigate. Nor have we worked to thoroughly understand the costs to students that result from our expectation that they perform "smartness" in particular, white-normed ways. It is our job, not that of students, to understand that they are struggling under the weight of these impossible expectations. It is our job as educators to understand these potential challenges. It is our job as educators to provide spaces for students to talk to us and with each other about them. It is our job as educators to work harder to foster environments that are supportive of all racially minoritized students. Ultimately, this is my hope for the racial opportunity cost framework and its power as a tool to foster meaningful change.

ROC Talk: Racial Opportunity Cost (ROC) Concerns the Costs of Academic Success for High-Achieving Students of Color in Predominantly White School Contexts

Sudeshna Flores and Dr. Leslie Gonzales

A note from Terah Venzant Chambers: I am probably not supposed to have a "favorite" ROC Talk, but I don't mind saying that this comes close. Leslie Gonzales is my brilliant colleague and friend; Sudeshna Flores is her extraordinary daughter, whom I have had the pleasure to know and watch grow for many years. It was important to me to include a student perspective in the ROC Talks. Flores participated in a podcast I did for the Great Lakes Equity Center in 2020. Based on that work, I invited her to write a ROC Talk for this book. She elected to include her mother and the "conversation" that evolved is both a wonderful take on the ROC framework and, even more importantly, a beautiful testament to the love between a mother and daughter.

In this essay, a daughter and mother jointly reflect on the racial opportunity costs that they have incurred from their respective perspectives. This reflection, as it appears here, is the outcome of several dialogues (written and verbal).

Sudeshna Flores: My name is Sudeshna Flores. I go by Sue. I'm currently in tenth grade. I really enjoy learning about science, exploring the human brain, and discovering information about genetics. One thing I dread about learning or school is when I'm in a class that teaches from a single and very strict point of view. I enjoy learning about all sides of science, history, and writing, so when I'm forced to learn from only one person's point of view, it can feel dreadful. I love hanging out with my friends and just going out to eat, or hanging out at the movies or at the lake. I love visiting my family in Texas and New Mexico. I am very close to my grandparents, all my aunts, and uncles and cousins.

Leslie Gonzales: My name is Leslie; I am Sue's mom. I am also a professor, and when I introduce myself to my students, I often start off by saying "I am a working-class, Latina, first-generation college-student-turned-academic." It is really important to me, as Sue knows, to let students know about my biography in case they are also a person of color or a first-generation college student who needs a little encouragement.

Sue: Yes, my mom takes a lot of pride in letting her students know who she is, and really who her whole family is! She tells a lot of stories! (Laughter) So, Mom, about Dr. Chambers's idea of racial opportunity cost, or ROC: What do you think about it?

Leslie: Well, I can think about it, personally, and what it was like to grow up in a predominantly white farming town and school, where my teachers, although they were nice, did not necessarily know what to do with a smart, inquisitive little Latina in their classroom. My mom and dad, your Grandma and Grampo, especially Grandma, had spent a lot of time even before kindergarten teaching me letters, sounds, and numbers, and they instilled in me a deep love of reading since I was really tiny! But my teachers could not see that I was smart, and I attribute this to the fact that they did not see students, or even families, like me or like mine, as having potential, and so they just kind of let me be. I think I lost a lot of opportunities, so that is a personal and slightly different version of a cost. How about you? What do you think about ROC? We live in a mostly white town, and you go to a mostly white school, and one that is, I would say, highly resourced. What are your thoughts about ROC?

Sue: When I think about ROC, I think about how you and Dad made the decision to leave South Carolina and come to Michigan because you were so worried about the schools there, or what my overall experience would be. I know you said that the schools in South Carolina were so poor. I remember we did not even have money at my school to have a computer lab, or to have science lessons. Remember, we used to have to take extra money if we wanted to do a hands-on science lesson?! However, I also remember that there were more kids of color at that school. I went to school with a lot of Black and Latino kids there, a lot of Asian kids too, and most of us were not rich, and probably there were many low-income families there, right?

Leslie: Yes, that is right.

Sue: Well, I know when Michigan State offered you the job, you looked at the schools here in Michigan, in East Lansing and in Okemos, and you saw that there were more resources. I think you also liked how it seemed that Michigan State was more involved in the schools and the teachers felt maybe more progressive? I am not sure.

Leslie: Yes, that is right. We definitely spent time looking at those things. Remember, we even talked with the counselors about the curriculum and teacher's freedom to be creative.

Sue: Yes, I kind of remember that part. I remember talking to the counselor. I was so small! (Sue was about 10 years old.) But this is an example of ROC to me. And ROC, it makes me feel disappointed, I know it's not the right thing. In my view, ROC shouldn't be the only path for kids of color to expand their knowledge in a good learning environment. What I mean is that students of color shouldn't have to give up, or risk, one thing, like being in a school with a lot of kids that look like them, and maybe get their cultural background more, in order to benefit and receive a good educational experience. We should get a good educational experience anywhere, without having to go through ROC.

Leslie: Yes, that is right. And to be honest, when I think about our decision-making process to come to Michigan and how we selected your school, I am slightly embarrassed and maybe a little regretful. I am not sure how to describe it. I feel like your dad and I leveraged our privilege, like our knowledge of how schools work and our money to buy in a certain neighborhood, in order to get you into a school that is really well-resourced and always highly ranked for its performance. We put you in that school rather than a school where there were more Kids of Color and where you might not be one of the very few Latina girls. I know the school we picked, it has not been super easy for you, and that is something that weighs heavily on me.

Sue: Well, yes, to be quite honest, my school is amazing, meaning there's a lot of opportunities and chances for students. And there are lots of resources for teachers or supervisors who are willing to take the time to help us out. However, that doesn't mean that I haven't experienced costs at my school. For example, all throughout my freshman year, I learned history from an extremely one-sided approach. I loved history, and I still do, I even enjoyed learning history while in my freshman year, but the only material we really used was our history books. Unfortunately, my teacher never really pushed for us to research beyond our books, and we were never open, or encouraged to have discussions. All of our materials were written by white authors, so that was the only perspective of U.S. history I learned throughout that year. But in reality, I knew there was so much more to learn and see beyond our outdated set of books. However, I think this is what the teacher was comfortable with, and so we were shortchanged, which feels a certain way when you are one of the only Kids of Color in the class, and then you are wondering why the history of your people, or your community is not really there, or why it is so short.

Another cost I've experienced is my surrounding classmates, or is based on the student body dynamic. My school is definitely not the most diverse, it's not all white students, but we don't have a large number of Black or Latino students. However, the Black and Latino students that we do have, we tend to stick together, in our own groups. I would say more than 90 percent of my friends are Black. There aren't too many Latinos, but I have found Latino friends in other schools. While my school claims we are diverse, the opportunities are different for students of color, which is close to what Dr. Chambers talks about in ROC.

It's not like opportunities are gone for Students of Color. They're not taken away, but they're definitely not as accessible or easy to find. It's almost as if they're hidden. The only way you'll really see them is if you're a Student of Color who fits the "perfect picture." If you're a Student of Color who excels in sports, doesn't cause a single ruckus, and seems "presentable," then you might make the list for receiving opportunities. The Students of Color who really stay true to themselves, and like to stay within their ethnic and racial friend groups, if we don't change how we look or dress a certain way, even if we do great in school, most likely the chances of opportunities won't reach us.

Leslie: Right. I have seen you balance these pressures, like wanting to access opportunities, but you also are really true to yourself and to who we are. You know, you are making me think of something that happens at work. Sometimes, at work, which you know, like most institutional settings, is predominantly white in terms of population and the culture, the norms there. There does not feel like there is room to be totally myself.

Sue: Yes! I mean, and so you kind of have to figure out how to get along in that setting, right. It is like, do you want to come in and be yourself? And I remember you like to wear your bright clothes, but you used to wonder if people thought you were "professional"! I am glad you still wear what you want and show up how you want! It is probably helpful to your students and other Women of Color who want to show up like that!

I mean, the thing is, when we have to figure out how to show up, it takes a lot of energy, and to be honest, I haven't always known I was smart. When I first switched schools, from South Carolina to my current school district, I realized how different it was and I sort of set an expectation for myself. I knew I wasn't going to do terribly, but I didn't think I was going to be an outstanding student in all my classes. It did not seem like I was smart in the way that these other kids were. I cared about other things, and I wanted to learn different things or maybe in different ways! So, I accepted that I was in it for the grades, not the learning.

Leslie: But it seems like you have had a turn in your thinking recently. Like since the summer of 2020, it seems like you have a different sense. What is this about?

Sue: Well, I think there are a few things. I really wanted to be smart, or feel smart, and when I started high school, I decided to try to change my attitude and I worked really hard in history, the same history class I mentioned earlier. I decided to take a risk and apply for AP History for my sophomore year. I went up to the teacher

> and said, "I know it seems like I am barely making my Bs and As for history, but I really like history, and if you look at my recent grades, you can see I have been getting As more consistently. I was hoping you could support my application for AP History next year." At my school, the teacher's recommendation is kind of the most important thing for getting into AP. We all know that is how it works. In fact, my friend (another Girl of Color) and I had the same conversation with this teacher. Well, in the end, we did not get in. We were rejected. You and I talked and I was disappointed, but you helped me get through it and I was ok. Then, COVID started and I had to do school online. I started exploring all these online resources outside of my class hours. I started to learn extra material or perspectives. I spent a lot of time learning from Creators of Color on TikTok, and they were talking about social and historical and political issues in a way that I have heard from you but never from young people, or other teachers! So, I started realizing this is the history I want to learn about! This was really important to me because I learned about institutional racism and I was able to understand how things work, like the police and the legal system and how they are all tied to slavery and anti-Blackness. I just had all these light bulbs going off.

Then, I got really, really lucky this year in school. What helped me realize I was actually smart was the handful of amazing teachers I've had this year! I had teachers who did a little extra to help push their students, or throw in facts and knowledge that were beyond our textbooks and learning curriculum, and then they were excited when I could give information beyond the textbook. The teachers who helped me realize how smart I am were the teachers who took the time to set up different methods or ways of teaching for me, whatever fit my brain best. Then, they would give me a little push, let me do all the work, and I realized I was smarter and more capable than I thought I was. I had my first Black teacher this year and she was amazing, a total Queen. She made me see that I am actually really good at math! I also had a woman science teacher who was so excited by all the questions I asked her in chat and in email. It was like she was so excited to have me ask questions, and I was not a bother. I became really interested in genetics and brain research in her class, but I think also because we have a lot of dementia in our family, and she let me explore all these questions. Also, I had a literature teacher and a history teacher that encouraged us to talk about history and social issues in a really different way. In my literature class, I wrote a paper on racism in medicine and in history, I did projects and always pointed out how short-sighted or white-washed the textbook was. I applied for AP History for next year and got in based on my work. So, I guess I am saying that having the freedom to explore ideas that I knew were out there and having teachers that were excited to let me explore was really key. However, it makes me sad because I know I just lucked out. My friends have not had the same experience, and I know one time one of my best friends, who is Black, kind of had to explain why the Derek Chauvin verdict was correct, and it is not that she had to explain it, but how the teacher put her in that position. So, that is maybe another cost, right? Like, even though I am doing and feeling better now, even if I don't totally "fit" the perfect picture, some of my friends are still going through it. So, we talk a lot about this stuff. We talk about it and help each other out, and I am very clear that I experience the world and school and teachers differently probably because I have this light-skin privilege that my Black friends don't have. It is a lot to carry, actually.

Leslie: This is important. How do you think this is a particular kind of ROC? I mean, I have ideas, but I think Dr. Chambers would want to hear from you.

Sue: Well, the white kids probably are not thinking about how they have privilege in the same way, even when they do think about their privilege! For example, I want to be sure that if I am hanging out with my friend group and we get in trouble, or there are cops around, I want to be sure I am prepared and ready to step in and make sure that my Black friends are not having to interact with the cops because we don't trust them, to be honest. And it hurts me to know that my friends have to carry this extra fear, or to be so careful and walk on eggshells. It is how, I have learned, racism works. It is like it keeps us all so busy and worried and careful that you cannot just live. I have to do my part, like you say, use my privilege when and how I can. It is not like being a white savior (laughter) but is more like standing by your community.

Leslie: You remind me of the importance of coalition, which means working with people across groups, across racial, ethnic, gender, or class groups in order to be in solidarity. It is really important work, hard work, but really important.

Sue: Yes, I think it is. I am really glad we are going to end on this note, because it gives me hope. The costs are there, but so is the hope. I am also really hopeful for teachers and TikTok or social media creators that give us the space to learn.

Terah Venzant Chambers's Take

There is so much richness in the dialogue between Sue and her mother, Leslie. Sue is so skilled at talking about her experience moving from an under-resourced school in South Carolina to a well-resourced school in Michigan. That move came with a number of additional challenges, though. As she talked through those constraints, she said, "We should get a good educational experience anywhere, without having to go through ROC," which really is the central thesis of the racial opportunity cost framework. Black students should not, for example, be put on display in the way Sue's classmate was, expected to defend the court's decision to hold Derek Chauvin accountable for the murder of George Floyd.

I was also taken by Sue's discussion of not being accepted into an AP History course—not even allowed to try—because of the school's requirement to have a teacher recommendation to take the course. Luckily for her, she had additional time in her high school career to take the course later and was encouraged by her mother and by subsequent teachers to explore topics of interest to her. By turning to social media and other platforms where she could access information about the history of minoritized people that resonated with her, her passion for history exploded and her grades improved, leading to her being able to take the AP History class a year after she first tried. This is a testament to Sue's resilience and inner strength as well as the support and encouragement she received from her parents and key teachers. However, we know from the stories of students in the ROC project that not all students have this same sense of self-determination that would allow them to persevere through a challenge like a teacher telling them they cannot take an AP class. However, Sue stood out for her ability not to let this barrier hold her back.

The final point I take from Sue's part of the conversation was the role that key teachers played in her experience—the Black teacher (a "Queen," as Sue said) who ignited her love for math and a few others who supported her exploration of topics of personal resonance for her and broader issues of social justice and equity. I think this is an important reminder that even in schools that have entrenched racialized norms for success, as Sue's seemed to have, these pockets of relief were present. It is possible to create these spaces and then work to expand them so they are not so isolated to particular teachers or classes. As Sue reminded us at the end of her essay, there is hope.

There are also a few points I want to raise from Leslie's part of the conversation. The first is the exchange between her and Sue about performative expectations. When Sue seemed to struggle to provide an example of these expectations, Leslie stepped in to share an example of her own struggles as an adult meeting expectations in the higher education space she occupied—wondering if wearing bright colors or other stylistic preferences that aligned with her cultural traditions were "appropriate" for the white-normed spaces of higher education. This provides a peek into the future-oriented and larger opportunities for the ROC framework that I will expand on in the conclusion to this book.

Another aspect to raise from Leslie's comments was her feeling "embarrassed" or even "regretful" that she and her partner put Sue in a school that was well-resourced but that also set her up to experience racial opportunity cost. Her story reminded me of Lolita's ROC Talk and the mixed feelings she had about selecting a school for her girls given the experiences she had as a K–12 student. There is no right answer, of course—at least not for parents of racially minoritized children. As I note throughout the book, all schools are imbued with these racialized expectations regardless of their demographics. The racial opportunity cost is perhaps more pronounced in predominantly white schools, which is why students who attended those schools might have experienced more distinct struggles. But even students who attended more racially diverse schools or schools located in urban areas experienced ROC. Further, students who attended schools with fewer resources, like Emma, certainly also faced their share of struggles. Knowing this will not likely help parents like Leslie or Lolita (or me, to be honest) escape the sense of responsibility we feel sending our precious young children into school environments that take so much from them. That is a hard reality to accept. However, I am encouraged by the bright spots in the stories students shared and knowing that there are ways to make schools less costly for racially minoritized students. Most of all, I look at the example set by students like Sue and I know that if my son grows up to be a fraction as smart, kind, and self-assured as her, then I know that he will be just fine.

CHAPTER 3

Intersectional Factors[1]

> "She said if I wanted to speak Spanish to do it at my Spanish class," Vianery said. "It hurts, because I came to this country to accomplish my dreams, and to hear that—it's not fair."[2]

Students at Cliffside Park High School staged a walkout after a video surfaced that showed a teacher yelling at several students, including Vianery Cabrera, quoted above. Vianery said she was speaking with her friends in Spanish, "because that's how we feel more comfortable," when the teacher began yelling at them to "speak American." This news story seemed a fitting start to this chapter because it highlights the idea that while race is at the forefront of students' daily experiences, the intersection of their racial identity with other social identities cannot be ignored. These identities are woven together into the same fabric of who they are.

To that point, the language we speak is such a central aspect of identity. As Vianery said, she felt more comfortable speaking Spanish. Thus, when the teacher yelled at her to "speak American," her words were laden with meaning. Of course there is no such language as "American," but the teacher's reprimand was not really about that. Rather, the teacher was performing her role as reinforcer of racialized expectations, that white "imagination" to which Bonilla-Silva referred that "grants eternal objectivity to the views of elite Whites and condemns the views of non-Whites to perpetual subjectivity."[3] This sentiment is at the core of the teacher's admonishment; she saw the students' speaking Spanish as an affront to those deeply held beliefs even though there was nothing wrong with what Vianery did.[4] The teacher's comments fell into a long-standing history where immigrants to the United States were systematically "Americanized" through the school system, learning expectations that, similarly to the case with Vianery, had nothing to do with their academic success and in many instances were not designed to support their learning.

From Vianery's perspective and in light of the ROC framework, however, the teachers' comments were a significant blow to her sense of belonging in the school. She said that speaking Spanish helped her feel more "comfortable," but in this school that was not as important as her compliance with white logics. Speaking Spanish is not a specific aspect of racial identity. Yet, from Vianery's perspective, speaking Spanish was likely as much a part of her identity as was being Latina and being from the Dominican Republic. The racial implications of the encounter are clear but were tied into other aspects of Vianery's social identities. Her story helps elucidate why we must make room for this broader dimension of identity. Thus, ***intersectional factors*** are an important aspect of the ROC framework, helping flesh out the impact of the school environment on Black and Latinx students.

INTERSECTIONAL FACTORS

Researchers have documented what racially minoritized people know at an experiential level—that race continues to be salient in our U.S. society. I wanted to highlight that role within the ROC framework, which is why race is unapologetically centered in this work. However, other identities matter, too. This is not an "either/or" situation. Race matters and so do these other identities. Importantly, race works *with* these other identities. This idea of mutually reinforcing identities, what Kimberlé Crenshaw calls intersectionality, speaks to the synergy created by overlapping identities, such as race, class, gender, gender identity and expression, sexual orientation, language, ability, etc. While the core concept of racial opportunity cost focuses on students' racialized experiences, as we learned with Vianery's story, these are often deeply intertwined with students' other social identities. I want to share a few examples of how this mattered for the students with respect to their cultural/ethnic identity, language, gender, and social class and include a closing note about sexual orientation and gender identity/gender expression.

Cultural/ethnic identity

Although we invited students to identify themselves however they chose, collectively we often referred to them as "students of color" in all of our recruiting materials and interviews. This set up a critical exchange in the Latinx focus group about identity. Near the start of the conversation, Emma keyed in on our use of the term "person of color" to talk about her introduction to the term when she came to Northern College:

> The first time I heard "student of color," I jumped straight into thinking it was just one up from "colored students. . . ." No, I'm Puerto Rican. You know? 'Cause coming from the school with mostly Mexicans, if you got lost, they call you Hispanic. So, I was Latina. I was Latina and that's cool. And then I come here, and I am one with like international students. So, my identity just gets flushed out even more. And that bothered me because my Puerto Rican identity just means so much to me. So, being called a student of color and not being able to distinguish myself as Puerto Rican anymore was heartbreaking. That's everything that I have worked so hard to stay connected with and here it gets flushed out with just the general student, where anyone who has a hint of color on their skin can be [a "student of color"].

As Emma's words made clear, the students felt very connected to their cultural identities. While at the time of the interviews we used the terms "Latina" or "Latino," or "people of color" as a general category until we learned their preferences in terms of identity, these conversations became a catalyst for students to talk about the importance of their specific identities. This prompted Emma to talk about her own challenges in making her identity fit within prescribed categories. Her identity as Puerto Rican meant she was sometimes identified as an international student despite her family coming from a U.S. territory. She pushed back against group labels like "student of color," "Hispanic," or "Latina" because for her it erased her proud Puerto Rican identity. She identified as an ally to the other Latinx students in the project but did not want that to force her to change how she saw herself. Emma's clarification about her identity is a pertinent reminder that even as race can be a primary way of identifying, it may not fully encompass or represent how people see themselves. This point came through clearly in many of our conversations with students.

Another aspect that came up related to the salience of cultural identity and the norms associated with them had to do with connections with family, particularly the cultural expectations the students navigated. One such expectation that came up consistently for our Latina students in particular was the issue of moving away from home to attend college. In this exchange at the Latinx focus group at Northern College, Emma began talking about her family's expectation of her as a *señorita* not to leave the house until she was married:

> My parents are like, "Go to college, you can make it." My parents are like, "You need to be better than we were." That's what I had to go through. I can just imagine people whose parents don't encourage them in that way, you know? 'Cause leaving the family? You don't. I'm a señorita. You don't leave the house. You only leave the house when you are married with your husband to another house. This is the norm. This is what has always been told to me. . . . I have all these cousins [who went to college], but they all stayed home, I am the only one who's ever decided to leave.

Emma spoke about what a big deal it was for her to go away to college. Going to college was not the issue, as she had many cousins and other relatives who pursued a number of higher education degrees in various fields. However, they all went to college in the general metropolitan area where they lived, while Emma went to a college that was more than six hours away by car. Once Emma raised this issue in the group, Araceli joined in the conversation, adding her perspective on leaving home for college. Northern College was even farther from her home state of Tennessee:

> I can definitely agree with what [Emma] was saying. This is my whole thing. I mean, I can't tell you how many times I was in the car with my mom and we were going to the store and she just started crying. She's just like, "Araceli, I can't believe you are leaving me, do you not love me anymore, is that it?" 'Cause being here [at Northern College], you do get lonely. Especially with my family; we are so close. I'm used to waking up in the morning, we're making coffee, we're drinking it. We have a waffle maker, you know? We'll make a waffle, go to yard sales, whatever, you know? And it's just like, being here, I don't have that. I mean, there's nothing close to it. Garage sales, I don't even know if they have garage sales here. . . . And the thing with my parents, they didn't stay long [when they brought me to college]. I mean, they came, they dropped me off, and they left. And the reason: my dad, he's like, "I'm sorry, if I stay here, I am gonna take you back. So, I am just gonna leave." It's a fifteen-hour drive from here to [my home]. They didn't stop. They didn't stop until they got to Missouri and had to take a rest. It is heartbreaking.

I remember feeling Araceli's pain when she relayed this story and the emotion still comes across in her words here. Araceli was very close with her family, which she saw as an important aspect of her cultural heritage—her very being. Many of the students were close with their families and relied on them for support. Even Emma noted above that she saw her family's expectations as encouragement and could not imagine what it would be like not to have that backing. And, while their families were generally supportive of them, the idea of going away to college was an issue that several of the Latina students, in particular, discussed. It was an additional complexity that they navigated, and an important nuance to the ROC that they experienced as a result. According to the racial scripts in their schools, it was not enough just to *go to* college, but *going away* to college and attending what was perceived as a prestigious university seemed to be part of the expectations imbedded in their schools.

Language

Related to the aspect of cultural or racial identity was the importance of language, particularly for the students who identified as Latinx. Like them, Vianery felt most comfortable when she was speaking Spanish, as she said in the vignette that opened this chapter. Similar to Vianery's teacher who reprimanded her for speaking Spanish in class, Syril had an encounter with a teacher who required students to speak in English. He told us:

> One of my teachers [said] we [couldn't] speak in Spanish or any other language except English. And to me that's a blow to my culture. That's just what I speak, I mean, that's my language. But her argument was that you don't need to use it at school because at school you're supposed to speak English. . . . To me, that's like stripping culture. So, I mean I would have to abide by her rules; I just didn't agree with them.

Syril felt he had no power to do anything but follow the teacher's rules even if he felt that she was separating him from his culture in the process, reminiscent of the process described by Valenzuela in her work with Mexican American students. Carmen felt similar to Syril, that speaking Spanish was important to her. However, she did not feel the same constraint in her school environment, telling us:

> I spoke Spanish when I wanted to, you know, it was not like "I don't want to do. . . ." I never changed who I was because I wanted to fit in. Like to this date, I don't listen to music in English, and it doesn't affect anything, you know, so I don't feel I ever . . . like, I never hid that I was Hispanic.

Carmen felt that speaking Spanish was an important part of her identity. It helped her stay connected to her identity, and she never felt that she had to "change who [she] was" in order to be seen as successful in her school. She was able to represent her identity in the manner of her choosing without feeling that it would compromise her standing in her school. However, recall in an earlier chapter how other Mexican American students in her school were surprised by her success as a Latinx student, suggesting that her ability to make the decisions she did may have said more about her individual characteristics than it did about her school environment.

Addressing this issue from another perspective, Araceli shared with us that her parents were intentional about ensuring that she was proud of her language and heritage:

> The people that [my parents] knew, even they might not be here legally and they won't speak to their children in Spanish. And my parents just don't understand that. [My mom's] like, "Not only are they depriving them of their culture in a way, but they're also kind of holding them back from being able to learn more things." It was like, being bilingual you have so many advantages already, you know? And she's like, "Why can they not understand that?"

Araceli shared with us the influence her parents had on her as well as their frustration with other parents who did not provide that same cultural foundation for their children. When she said she and her parents did not understand other parents' decision to not provide their children with this foundation, they knew acutely that the decision came from a place of wanting their children to be successful, of recognizing the white logics that created little space for students not to conform. Araceli's parents were lamenting that this should be necessary because of how important that heritage was to them and, ironically, that the foundation of being bilingual and strongly grounded in their language and heritage would *enhance* students' academic success. It was devastating to them to think that the school would take that opportunity away from children. In that sense, Araceli and her parents were aligned with Carmen and Syril about the importance of language, specifically of speaking Spanish, in their experiences.

Social class

Social class was a fascinating variable in the students' experience because of its operation in relation to their peers. Most of the students we talked with came from working-class or middle-class backgrounds; however, they often attended school with white students from much more affluent backgrounds. Thus, navigating this aspect of their school environment created significant tension. Both Northern College and Southern College are elite private colleges with soaring price tags for tuition and room and board. Because of financial aid and other scholarships, the students in our study were rarely paying the full cost. However, there were certainly other students at the school whose families did not need any aid. For some of the students we spoke with, this was a new experience, as they came from high schools where most of their classmates came from similar economic backgrounds to their own. However, some of the students in the study had already been exposed to wealthy students in high school. For example, Rick, who attended an all-male private school, noted that he was used to going to school with wealthy white students:

> Going to a predominantly white high school, I think you kind of prepared for the culture shock. I know for me one of the biggest things that I noticed wasn't an issue of race but was socioeconomic factors. The majority population of students were [wealthy], so I guess I was prepared from high school to get that culture shock. So, going to school [here] with upper-class white students wasn't such a big deal to me. I was also kind of used to having that small, tight-knit minority community because I had seen it in high school, as well.

Rick suggested that it was social class, not race, that he most noticed about his experiences with his peers. I did not take this to mean that he thought racial identity was not important, but that the social class disparities were just that polarizing. From that perspective, it is easy to see how these issues were intertwined, as he noted that the affluent students were overwhelmingly white and the small community of racially minoritized students with which he identified had a social class background more similar to his. He went on to clarify just how extreme the wealth disparities between himself and his white classmates were, telling us:

> Race alone was not the only interesting thing about my high school. It was also the socioeconomic aspect of it. These are kids who junior year, they get a car. They're driving their daddy's Lexuses to school, whereas [my family says,] "Here. You can borrow the car once in a while. But no. You're not *getting* the car." Or, here's the kids who [say], "Oh, where you goin' for spring break?" "Oh, I'm goin' to Cancun." "Oooh, I'm stayin', I'm stayin'. I'm gonna be sitting with my grandmother, watching TV and stuff." I mean, I can't say that I grew up in a completely impoverished community. But I know what it feels like to be lower income.

Rick confirmed the salience of race *and* class in his school. From his perspective, his family was not poor, but it felt that way compared to the affluent students with whom he went to school. Micayla shared a similar perspective about the significant income disparities at her public high school located in one of the most affluent areas in Houston:

> [My high school] was so diverse because you had people [at] the bottom of the socioeconomic ladder and people way up at the top. I know this one guy who went to [my high school], we went to middle school too and he was like, I got my own wing in the house now. He has his own wing in a house with a maid's quarter. It's like, he has his own wing. That's . . . that's crazy. And it's just, you know, it's stuff like that. We can't even really comprehend him. 'Cause you have such diversity of people and it kind of led to a lot of clashes, but generally, the people wouldn't interact because you would be separated.

Like Rick, Micayla went to school with very wealthy students. It was not just that they had a little more money, but it was a level that was impossible for her to "even really comprehend" both because it was so different from her own experiences and because of the segregation that occurred in her school. Micayla shared that a "school within a school" existed and described how students were separated into different tracks: the most elite classes were reserved mainly for wealthy white students, and Black students were put in lower-level courses to "get them out of the way." This set up a situation where she and the other Black students who were in advanced classes were still figuratively separated from the wealthy white students, which perhaps ironically created more flexibility for her to create community with other Black students in different tracks. Despite sharing the same physical space with the wealthy white students, the income differences created a symbolic gap; at the same time, she was physically separated from other Black students although she had more in common with them. This wealth dynamic set up a different context in her school from other students in our project, although it did not insulate her from experiencing racial tensions.

While Rick and Micayla saw daily the ways in which income disparities differently impacted the experiences of their wealthy white classmates, other students only saw those differences outside their school walls. For example, Carla had never considered the status of her Chicago public school until she was able to visit a suburban school not far away.

> As far as education, I had the opportunity to visit some really good high schools. I would walk through the hallways, like, "Man, they have real walls." They have good things to do and their classes are really intense, they really work. I would question myself, I mean, I'm doing well in high school, but what does that mean? What is my high school compared to this rich, funded high school? They have all these great opportunities, chances to study abroad—like, that never occurred to me. What is study abroad? I never even thought about going out of the country.

Carla was not aware that her school lacked resources relative to those located in more affluent areas. She became aware of the disparities when she visited a wealthy school in the suburbs that "had real walls," and study abroad programs, and other opportunities that were not available in her school—indeed, that she did not even know were possible. I was struck by her characterization that the students in that school "really work," since I knew how hard she had studied in order to get into Northern College. My sense was that more than objectively knowing that the students in that suburban school worked harder, she constructed this narrative in part based on her internalization of white logics that associate proximity to whiteness as inherently better. Regardless of what drove her perspective, the experience had her questioning her own academic success in her high school, given that students in this well-funded school had access to opportunities she did not.

Like Carla, Ice was not exposed to substantive income disparities in his own high school; there were ranges in students' social class background, but nothing like what Rick and Micayla experienced. Unlike Carla, it was not until Ice got to college that he began to realize just how different his wealthier Northern College classmates' experiences and opportunities were from his own:

> I got here, and it was like I didn't really *know* it until I get here, and I'm the only one without a laptop. And then, people keep asking me, "Why don't you have a cell phone? Why don't you have a cell phone?" I'm like, "Well, my mom's not gonna buy me a cell phone." Like, it's that kinda thing. And then, you start to realize. But it's only because of the way that other people live that you see it. So, it's kinda the same thing. . . . And maybe, that's a big issue because people are comin' from all these different classes. And now, you're [really] seeing because when you're growing up, everybody around you's basically kinda the same. Like, you're in this environment where if you're middle class, everybody in your class is probably middle class, lower class, upper class. But you get here, it's like big m-m-mush, mush of everybody. So, that's where those issues come up.

Ice made a point similar to Micayla, that these class disparities created tension when students from such different class backgrounds were in the same space. The students made clear that these income disparities, while jarring in themselves, were also responsible for fostering additional challenges for the students to overcome. Seeing the resources other students had had fostered feelings that they were not as well prepared or did not belong in these elite college environments. For Ice, students asking why he did not have a laptop or cell phone fueled a sense of unease about his status at the college. Further, because almost without exception the affluent students were white and the racially minoritized were not, a racial dynamic came into play.

Gender

We knew from previous research that gender likely influenced the students' experiences, and so we were intentional about asking them directly about the role of gender in their experiences. It was thus not a surprise when the students confirmed its salience. What was unexpected, however, was the near unanimous acknowledgment that the Black and Latinx young men had more difficult experiences. Speaking to this issue, Gregg, who went to a high school in north Texas, talked about the issues he navigated back in his hometown:

> High school actually got a lot more serious for me because once we got the IB program, the numbers started really high for African Americans, particularly males. And then it dwindled as we went on, particularly a lot freshman year to sophomore year. [One reason was] because a lot of my friends were still military and they moved out. Then it came down to like five of us and three dropped. They said they didn't want to do it. They were sick of it and they didn't get along with our teachers, which none of us really did at that point in time.

A few of Gregg's comments drew my attention. First, he asserted that the number of Black males in the IB program "started really high" and then declined. This is a pattern across many schools, where racially minoritized students may start in advanced classes and then move out as time goes on. Sadly, his "really high" number was really probably seven or eight at the most, though I did not ask him specifically. However, since the numbers ended up being so small, even seven or eight would have seemed like a significant number. Also, I noticed that in his characterization of why students left, he did not say anything about their inability to be successful. Rather, they either left because of family military assignments (he lived near a military base) or "didn't want to do it" because they were tired of dealing with teachers who gave them trouble, or were otherwise pushed out. Elsewhere in his interview, he talked about how sports created a pathway for him, but that was not even enough to put him on a pathway to success. He made a conscious decision—part of the inner strength showcased at the beginning of this chapter—to do well academically. From his perspective, most of the other Black male students in his school were not able to do the same.

While Gregg noted the ways in which teachers made it more difficult for Black males to be successful, Zion talked about the pressures of navigating the white logics of his high school as a Black male, notably that there were particular negative performative pressures with which he dealt:

> 'Cause like, it wasn't considered cool to be a smart kid, or whatever. Like, that wasn't a really, uh, good quality. I don't know how you wanna put it. But … um … so like, I would do my work, but I wouldn't make it seem like [I was] always doing work or like I was always studying or whatever.

Zion noted that it was not "cool" to be a smart, Black young man. In order to pursue success, he felt it was necessary to play down his achievement, choosing not to carry books to class or study in front of other students. The racial scripts of his school environment did not create a pathway for him to be open with his success, and so playing it down was the only way for him to be successful. Ice spoke even more directly than Zion about the restrictive gender norms he encountered.

> It all turns out to be like, "College is bad. Play basketball." That's what I feel like. "Don't read." "You should probably try to rap." "It's cool to sell drugs." Like, that kind of stuff. And the thing is, it's an addictive kind of thing. Like, I've always listened to hip-hop. I love basketball. I've always hated reading. But because I've always put it in perspective, like, that's not real. That's not real. The chances of me becoming a basketball player are very slim. It's just like they have no chance at it. If a Black kid could really understand what one in a million really means.

It was confusing for Ice to feel like the messages he received about what he should strive for were things that he liked, like music and basketball. However, as he said, he also felt it was not "real" and so he was not deterred from his focus on school. He struggled to navigate the pressures of being a Black male who liked school but also liked things that were seen as stereotypical of Black males, like basketball and hip-hop music.

Perhaps it was not surprising to hear from the boys that they felt that they had it harder than girls; however, the girls expressed their belief that it was more difficult for the boys, too. In fact, their insight was perhaps more enlightening about why the situation was more difficult for boys. Micayla spoke to this directly, noting that there was a "dividing effect" that the boys faced that the girls did not.

> I think gender helped me more because it's ok to be a smart Black person, a smart Black female. Like, that's not as bad as being a Black male, a smart Black male who's on that kind of track. And so, I think that was the difference and that didn't have much as an ostracizing affect or a dividing effect that it had on the Black men.

Micayla was clear that as difficult as it may have been for her to navigate success in her school, her gender was not something that contributed to the challenge. The young men around her dealt with an "ostracizing effect" that was not applicable to her. Likewise, Jessica made a comment that aligned with what Micayla told us. Similar to Gregg's point about the dwindling numbers of Black men in advanced classes, Jessica noted that there were not many Black young men in her classes.

> It was very rare for a Black male to be in those classes, at least in my school. There weren't really very [many] high-achieving Black males in our school. Unless you were like [this one student] who graduated before us who was really exceptional, and everybody loved him. Unless you were like that, [and] most weren't. I heard stories that some people who were in regular classes used to be in the advanced classes in middle school. But they didn't take honors classes [in high school].

Jessica pointed out that only a truly exceptional Black male student was able to navigate the advanced classes in the school. She noted that there were students in advanced classes in middle school, but once they got to high school, they were not interested in taking the advanced classes. Again, she did not indicate that they were not capable of taking those classes, only that they chose not to take them. That the only Black male student who did well was "exceptional" and someone who "everybody loved" is a high bar for students to meet. Interestingly, it was Emma who provided the nuance we were looking for regarding the impact of gender on the students' experiences. As she explained:

> You would be lucky to be a boy and make it out alive at my high school. Simply put. You were lucky to be alive and finish high school. You either got jumped all the time—so many [of my] friends should not be alive right now. I thank God every day that they are, but they should not [be]. Guns have been put to their heads, they've been mugged, they've been robbed, they've been jumped, group jumped, groups [were] planning to kill them. . . . And guys did end up in emergency rooms all summer. [A friend who was shot that summer] could have died. He *should* have died. They took really good care of him. Right before junior year. I came back and I remember writing notes to him. I'm just like, "Look. Revenge. I know it's something you want. It's something I want to get for you. But revenge is you getting that diploma and continuing to get that next diploma that no one thinks you can get. And that's your revenge." And he's in college right now, but like, who would have told him that? Where are the other people who would have told him that?

Emma always had a way of making the complicated clear. She described just how difficult it was for the young men in her school to navigate their lives *safely*, let alone to achieve academic success. It was critical to understand how so many of the young men of color in our project were dealing with the intersections of race and gender in order to get a full sense of their experiences. This was a point Gregg raised, too when he talked about the pressure he felt not to fall into a stereotype:

> It's like, I want to be the strong Black man who's there and fits that strong Black man role, who eventually, when he gets there, he is going to provide for his family and be there for his kids and all that lovely great stuff that all our great Black leaders have done. And at the same time, I don't want to have to deal with every time I say something to you, every time I say something to you, whether I say it with an attitude and we're sitting across the table at lunch and I say, "I didn't agree with statement" [you say,] "Oh, Gregg." "Calm down, Gregg." And I've gotten that at [Southern College]. We're having a simple conversation and, I mean, it's getting loud. It's lunch! We're getting loud. It's like, "Hold on, hold on. I don't agree with that at all." "Are you ok? Are you alright?" And then somebody'll come and it'll happen to be a white girl or something. She'll come and she'll put her hand on my shoulder like, "Are you ok?" "Get off of me! I'm

> just fine. I just want to talk to this man about what he just said to me." And I sit up and I'll be the man. "Oh, he's being aggressive, we better end the conversation." It's just like. . . . [Big sigh] Damn it. You are going to hear what I got to say, you're going to go sit down. And she's watching me. [Big sigh] I can't win. I can't win for losing. And that's the problem I deal with to this day. How do I balance all of this? How do I balance being an educated Black man, a strong Black man, for my strong Black woman, and not come off [as] crazy to every other race that I come in contact with?

Gregg struggled with wanting to meet the standards of being the "strong Black man" but was frustrated that white people, especially white women, felt threatened by the emotion and passion he expressed. He felt that there was no way out of that situation, that he could not "win for losing."

While the students felt that the young men, particularly Black young men, had a more difficult path navigating the white logics in school, they did speak to some of the pressures faced by the young women. For example, Ice told us about his sister's struggles to pursue her dreams to go to art school in Switzerland. He said that his family's response was, "That's ridiculous. You a girl. You can't be walking around Switzerland with paints and stuff. Somebody's gonna eat you alive." Thus, it was not that students felt that the young women did not face their own challenges, just that from their perspective, the young men navigated a harder path. Elsie also talked about the additional constraints she faced from her family, particularly in going so far away for college:

> When I told my parents that I was leaving the state, I think they had a concern. They understood that they taught me well enough to make good decisions, but they always have that fear of "what happens if something happens to her? Especially since she's on her [own]." Like, "Oh, my little girl. I don't want anything happening to her." And, I mean, that's understandable.

Similar to some of the experiences shared by the Latina participants, Elsie similarly navigated cultural expectations that made leaving home to attend college far away a big deal. While the pressures that the young women faced may have been different from what the young men faced, they were pressures, nonetheless.

Sexual orientation

As the stories show, our conversations with the students were rich and dynamic. That said, there were times when our relatively short relationship-building time impacted the fullness of the conversations we had with students. One place where this was noticeable was in discussions of students' sexual orientation. While we asked students about their experiences with race and gender specifically, we also asked about other social identities that were salient to their experiences. Social class was an issue that came up, both directly in response to this question, but also indirectly in conversations about other topics. While we knew that there were very likely some students who identified as LGBTQ+, this was not something that any student raised directly. However, there were some interesting points raised about the intersection of sexual orientation with the students' navigation of their schools' racial logics in that students expressed being *perceived* as being gay for being smart. Speaking to this issue, Emma talked about her family suspecting she was a lesbian because she did not express any interest in dating, like her younger sisters. She brought this up in the conversation at the Latinx focus group at Northern College, telling the group:

> I didn't really, like, date, like my sisters. . . . And so, my grandmother interpreted this as me being a lesbian. She pretty much put me in therapy because of this.... She told the therapist, "Well, she—she's into her studies. She's like—she's not liking girls, but she's not dating. I—I mean, if she's a lesbian, I'll accept her." First of all, that's a lie. [Group laughter] She really is, like, one of the biggest homophobes out there. And she tries to pretend that she's so open. Granted, I'm not a lesbian, but because I came home talking about my female teachers in the way that I did, she just assumed something was going on there. But my brother would come home and talk about his teachers—granted not, like, how much they knew, but, "Oh, wow this teacher is really cute, or whatever." It's like, "Oh, you got a crush!" It was more of a joking matter. But [for] me, it's like, "You must be a lesbian 'cause you're not seeing any guys and you're talking about your [female] teachers."

Emma was clear that she did not identify as gay, but it was one way her grandmother tried to make sense of her not displaying interest in dating, like her siblings. Emma shared that while her grandmother indicated that she would be accepting of her if she were gay, Emma thought that her grandmother was only saying that to look good in front of the therapist.

Carla made a similar point. Again, although she did not identify as a lesbian, she told us that she was nonetheless seen that way by others. She shared a story about a guy she knew being seen as heterosexual because he thought that his female teachers were "cute." However, even though she never talked about being attracted to any teachers, male or female, people assumed she was a lesbian because she talked so positively about her female teachers. She told us:

> I never once even remotely said that I had a crush on my teacher—female or, like, whatever. But it was assumed because I would go on and on about all the different teachers and what I learned from them on that day. And it was just like, "Yep, lesbian."

Similar to Emma, there was no room in the racialized expectations she navigated for her to just be interested in learning. Thus, Carla felt that those close to her interpreted her going "on and on" about what she learned from her teachers to mean that she was gay. In this way, it is interesting to see how *perceived* identity came into play in some students' experiences. This underscores the point that in some of these cases, students' actual identities mattered less than how they were perceived. This was true not only for sexual orientation, but potentially for all of their social identities. This is reminiscent of the students' conversations about being perceived as acting white regardless of their personal identities. In this way, students' social identities were very much tied into the performative aspects of their school cultures.

Ice did not tell us that people thought he was gay, but he did share his thoughts about the ways in which pressures to conform to typical postures of masculinity might be removed for gay young men. He said:

> Once you know you're gay in high school, all those pressures are gone. You don't even have to fight [the pressures] anymore. So, you can just go with academics and be like, "This is my way outta here."

Ice did not suggest that being gay would make the pathway easier generally, but that the pressures that heterosexual Black men had to navigate in order to conform to expectations were different. From his perspective, pursuing academics might actually alleviate the pressure to conform. He noted that there were more out Black gay men at Northern College than at his high school, and he wondered if it was because it was a way, in his words, to "fight" the pressures. Knowing what we do about the salience of sexual orientation in other research and in my experience working with students outside of this research project, sexual orientation would absolutely play a critical role in the racial opportunity cost that students experience. I wish we had had more space and a greater opportunity to talk about this with the students in the project. I hope that future research will take this up.

In this chapter, students shared stories about the aspects of their identities that impacted their experiences in school. Race still featured prominently in each story. From students identifying closely with their cultural heritage and/or language, or navigating social class differences or the impact of gender, each of these social identities were deeply intertwined with their racial identity. Thus, while it is important to tease out these fuller aspects of social identity, they must be understood within the context of—as intersectional with—their racial identity.

ROC CLOSING THOUGHTS

One of the difficult aspects of the idea of intersectionality is seeing the interconnection, the complexity of social identities. It is not just about looking at gender *and* sexual orientation *and* language, etc. Rather, it is looking at the role of all of those identities together, synergistically. For example, I have shared stories throughout this book that Ice told us about his racialized experiences. The intersection of race with his other identities came through to some degree. However, in this chapter, I was able to focus more specifically on that broader perspective: that he was also dealing with the additional layer of social class that led his white peers at Northern College to ask questions about why he did not have a cell phone or a laptop. He was also working through expectations around gender expression that most of the students agreed made the path to academic success tougher for Black males than for other students. But even that perspective was complicated by the role of sexual orientation and his thoughts that Black men who identified as gay might have found that while that identity created challenges, it freed them from restrictive gender norms that heterosexual, cisgendered Black men might have faced. Most of all, it was important to take a moment in a book where I look at the experiences of "Black and Latinx" students to make space for the multidimensionality of their experiences. For example, to show that while Emma identified as Latinx for the purposes of our study, her identity as Puerto Rican was central to how she saw herself and sometimes caused tension with other Latinx students in her school. And, as her relationships with other Latinx students became strained and she identified more with her teachers, her peers and family started asking questions about her sexuality. All of these issues were rooted in the same racialized expectations, but there were also expectations that had similar roots in heteronormative, cisgendered, ableist, dominant culture. The central point is that in a book where I am cautioning us to expand our conceptions of what it means to be "smart" or "high-achieving" and to cultivate school norms that are not so costly for Black and Latinx students, it would be deeply problematic for me to present the experiences of the students in this project as monolithic. I stand by the salience of race. Furthermore, it is just as important to understand the wholeness of students' identities so that we can better support them. As Vianery said in the story that opened this chapter, as a recent immigrant to the United States from the Dominican Republic, speaking Spanish helped her feel "more comfortable." While school may never be a space where all students will feel completely at ease, we can proactively work to ensure that we foster environments where students are free to express the multitudes of who they are.

ROC Talk: Reflections from a Former Teacher

Dr. Courtney C. Mauldin

A note from Terah Venzant Chambers: Courtney Mauldin and I first met when she was considering doctoral programs. She was determined to make a purposeful move from the classroom to graduate school in order to better support students and teachers from minoritized backgrounds. I was delighted when she chose Michigan State and selected me to serve as her advisor. Mauldin played such an important role with the work on racial opportunity cost (and beyond that, truly became a part of our family) by helping translate this deeply theoretical work in a manner that would resonate with practitioners, particularly with some grant work that I undertook with the Great Lakes Equity Center. This ROC Talk is actually an adaptation of a podcast we did on ROC and the Black Lives Matter Movement (a podcast in which Sudeshna Flores from a ROC Talk appearing earlier in this book participated). To the degree that ROC resonates with K–12 teachers and school leaders, I have Courtney to thank.

As a former teacher in the elementary context, I often think about the ways that I witnessed my students and their parents navigate racial opportunity costs. They were present in the everyday of their school lives. While we were a pretty diverse school, with over 30 languages represented and a wealth of cultures, there were costs that I knew students incurred. For example, the fact that all the teachers didn't look anything like them, apart from maybe me and a few others. And our school interpreters were only equipped to assist with Spanish and Arabic. Keep in mind this is a school with 1,600 students and over 30 languages represented. It makes you wonder, where were students able to see themselves and their cultures, traditions, and practices reflected?

I think that a lot of times, what I saw as a trend was seeing how international fairs and things like that would happen and celebrate, you know, "culture." Don't get me wrong, I created the professional learning community (PLC) for culturally responsive classrooms that put this event on, but it was always a "first step" that I felt I had to take as a teacher to get buy-in from my school principal and resistant teachers. What I really wanted was for teachers to stop using harmful rhetoric in our school about students, to stop labeling them and calling them "504s" instead of their name. That PLC was something I wanted to create so that we could actually "do the work" of culturally responsive classrooms for all of our students. To me, that would have meant that all of our students felt seen and honored, not just celebrated once a year.

I think that what was also hard for me to reckon with is that for our Black students, there was nothing in place to necessarily celebrate or affirm their Blackness. This was the case for students who came to that International Fair, for sure. So, it left a lot of my kids wanting to be Other. And not "Other" in terms of just white, but Other in terms of anything else, so that they could feel equally special. And I think that was really hard to see. Seeing that firsthand makes me think about why we have to affirm that their lives matter in multiple ways in the classroom. At that level, but also at a school level. The district has to take some lead on that, too.

Terah Venzant Chambers's Take

In the ROC project, we heard repeatedly from students about the impact of having so few (or any) teachers of color. Courtney brings the teacher perspective in to the mix. Her thoughts made me think a bit differently about the importance of intersectionality factors, that by cutting students off from expressing the fullness of who they are, it might have the effect of taking away their feeling of "specialness," as Courtney described it. I am also taken with her expression of students feeling like just being "Black" was not special, that they were looking for ways to distance themselves from that feeling. There are so many ways that we do not help students feel that sense of pride in their racial identity: we try to "ignore" race—but in reality, we foster students' sense of shame or even lead them to internalize negative associations with their racial identity. Existing curricula tend to focus on negative or sorrowful experiences, particularly in Black history. And those realities are certainly there. But when we *only* teach about the brutalities of slavery or the challenges of school segregation, then we can unwittingly teach students that there is nothing positive about their history. Given how much the Black community and other minoritized groups have contributed to American history, this oversight is not only ahistorical but is dangerously misleading.

CHAPTER 4

Capacity Factors

> If we want students to act in ways that will maximize their future opportunities—to persevere through challenges, to delay gratification, to control their impulses—we need to consider what might motivate them to take those difficult steps.[1]

For a few years, it seemed like everywhere I turned, teachers and school leaders were talking about helping their students build grit and resilience, or what some scholars began calling "non-cognitive variables."[2] One day, I scrolled through my social media feed and found the excerpt above, from an article in *The Atlantic*, espousing the importance of grit. I had an immediate negative reaction to seeing yet *another* person suggesting that if students could just "control their impulses," then they could "maximize their future opportunities." The idea of the power of building resilience in students was popularized by Angela Duckworth, particularly her Ted Talk, which, last time I checked, had over six million views on YouTube.[3] In my experience, an idea that resonates with many educators is that even beyond family income, IQ, or how safe a student feels, "grit" stands out as a critical factor in success. A few things strike me about this message about resilience, mostly the focus on children and what *they* need to do. If only *they* were more future-oriented or *they* could better control their impulses, success would follow.

In line with deficit thinking–oriented literature, messages about grit and resilience seemed to focus solely on the child and not on other factors that are more within the school's control. Even saying "school's control" is not telling the complete story, as there are often issues outside of a particular school's direct control that are important to consider in this conversation, like a lack of resources to purchase updated curricular materials, update learning spaces, or hire and retain experienced teachers. Worse, the gains that result from focusing on these student-level factors may justify not addressing the larger challenges some schools face. Never mind that our teachers are piecing together curricula using YouTube videos to supplement their twenty-year-old social studies textbooks—if only the students would be more resilient!

I share this background on grit and resilience to start this chapter because this discourse may seem to align with the argument I make about racial opportunity cost; however, there are some important cautions. The point is not to ignore resilience or minimize its salience in helping students achieve success. Rather, it is critical to understand how these skills *are a response to* the school environment and reflect on too-large numbers of students who are not able to use their "grit" to overcome the racialized challenges they face in their school environment. While the central relationship in the racial opportunity cost (ROC) framework is between the school environment and the individual student, understanding these non-school factors, what I call ***capacity factors,*** is a critical role in that fuller calculation.

CAPACITY FACTORS

As noted above, capacity factors are aspects of students' immediate environment that are not under the school's control that influence Black and Latinx students' ability to navigate factors that contribute to the ROC they experience. In general, these were issues that had a positive impact; so, another way to think about them would be protective factors. They explain why two students who attend the same school environment or come from the same family may experience different ROCs. Capacity factors included issues that were internal to the students themselves, like resilience or a sense of inner-strength. However, other non-school factors also played an instrumental role in the students' experiences—most notably, students' families and/or nonprofit mentoring programs. Each of these areas is taken up in greater depth in this chapter.

Student-level capacity factors

Reading any of the students' stories so far, one cannot help but see how amazing the students were. We learned this when we met them, but their personalities certainly still come across even on the words on these pages. It was clear that the same qualities that endeared us to them were also an important part of what allowed them to persevere in their school environments despite the challenges they faced. These personality traits included a sense of resilience, but more than that, an internal fortitude or inner strength that helped them move forward. One of my favorite quotes that shows this aspect in the students came from Emma, whose experience with a teacher laughing at her when she said she was planning to attend Harvard appears in an earlier chapter. This would have been a crushing experience for me as a student. However, Emma took it as a challenge, thinking to herself, "I'll prove you wrong just like I proved everyone else wrong!" Emma and many of the students in our project had a similar sense of wanting to prove they could be successful, the challenges they faced serving to fuel their determination that much more. Many of the students were not shy about their own role in their success. For example, Adriana noted that she only had herself to motivate her. She told us:

> I just, I did it. I wanna say that my education and what I've done to get me here right now, I did it more for a personal reason. It wasn't because like people at my school motivated me. . . . But, I wanna say [that's] also motivation. Like, I did it because I don't have a Plan B. I can't drop out and go to my mother or go to a house. It's kind of like after college, I'm on my own. And I feel that that plays a part.

For Adriana, the fact that she did not perceive any support coming from her school motivated her to do well. She relied on herself because she did not feel that she had a backup plan. She also had the support of individuals in third-party mentoring organizations who provided support. However, at the end of the day, she understood that she had only herself to rely on.

Gregg is another student whose stories have expressed an undercurrent of self-determination or self-efficacy. Thus, it should not be a surprise to learn that Gregg credited himself for his success. At the end of his interview, when we asked him if there was anything else about his experiences that we should know that would help us understand him better, he talked about his mindset:

> To be perfectly honest—and I try not to sound as cocky as possible—I think I was a really above and beyond driven type of individual. I mean, to work the three jobs and pay for my mistakes in high school as opposed

> to trying to put it off or something like that. And still want to do the stuff that I did or do the stuff I successfully did thus far, I think was truly a God-given talent and a gift from God for me to be able to do that. 'Cause I don't think that a lot of people can truly do that.

Gregg was not shy about sharing challenges that he'd faced in his younger years, getting in trouble and then making a conscious decision to use his intelligence to achieve his goals. And he was right. I do not know many people who would have been able to overcome the challenges that he did. We did not perceive Gregg as cocky at all, though he seemed aware that some people saw him in that way. Rather, he came across as self-aware and extraordinarily capable of not letting setbacks derail him from being successful. It was remarkable to see such a trait in a person so young.

Interestingly, while some students were aware of this ability in themselves, others maintained that there was nothing special about them to explain their success. At the end of our interview with Rita, we asked her the same question we had asked Gregg: Was there anything else we should know about her? She surprised us by talking about the email we had sent out through the Black student organization at her college to recruit students for our project.

> When I first heard [about] the project it sounded so weird to me. I was like "high-achieving African American?" 'Cause I just didn't see myself as that. I just went to [my magnet high school], took some classes, and now I am in college or whatever. I didn't really, I don't know. To me it sounded kind of pompous [to call myself a] high-achieving African American student. I was like, "Why would they care about that?" I was just, I don't know. I just saw myself as a regular ol' Joe. . . . I just see myself as trying to get an education.

Rita did not see herself as particularly unusual for her accomplishments, even going so far as thinking it was pompous to identify herself as high achieving. Yet, hearing her story of leaving most of her friends in her neighborhood to attend a prestigious magnet school and enduring the isolation she experienced there, it was clear that this was not a path that other students from her old school or who lived in her same neighborhood had attempted. She was about as far from a "regular ol' Joe" as I could imagine; however, her humility was an endearing part of her personality.

While for some students, like Adriana and Gregg (and, though reluctantly, even Rita), an internal personality trait contributed to their success, for others it was also a cultivation of particular skills. One of the skills students talked about was the ability to code-switch. Being able to appropriately mirror the expectations of a variety of different environments contributed to their ability to be successful. This was true for Zion, who was one of many who used the ability to code-switch to move in and out of various environments:

> Coming here [to Northern College], my speech like changes automatically and I can't really like change it back. So, it becomes a more proper and like, uh, a little more acceptable, or whatever. When I go home, or when I'm talking on the phone with my mom, it automatically changes to the way I would talk at home.

Code-switching was a protective factor that several students used to help navigate shifting expectations from one environment to another. Zion used that skill to cultivate close relationships with his family and friends back home and then transition smoothly to the different expectations at Northern College. The transition was not always perfect, though. Clashes occurred for him when environments and expectations overlapped, for example, while listening to music in his room where his white suitemates might hear. Nonetheless, code-switching was a skill he credited with helping him navigate these complex environments.

Whether it was the ability to code-switch or the general resilience to persevere through challenges, these factors internal to the students we talked with were instrumental in understanding how they were able to achieve success. And yet, these stories shared by Emma, Adriana, Gregg, Rita, and Zion all illustrated the point that building resilience alone does not tell the whole story. The rest of the story explains that they were resilient in a school environment that made their success an arduous journey. By extension, it is easy to see how other students who were just as capable of handling the academic rigor but lacked that same fortitude were not able to overcome the challenges. We got a glimpse of this from the focal students in this project about how other students in their school responded to the same environmental constraints. For example, Carmen shared in chapter 1 that she never felt that she "had to change who [she] was" to fit in with the racialized logics in the school, but another Mexican

American classmate demonstrated that despite her personal feelings, those racialized expectations still impacted Carmen and those around her. This revealed an important point about individual level capacity factors; while a student may possess individual traits that allow them to more successfully navigate these dominant normed expectations, this achievement does not negate the existence of those expectations. Thus, it is imperative that we work to foster school environments that do not require students to be so gritty in order to be successful. Resilience is a useful skill, but not to the exclusion of attention to institutional factors.

Family-level capacity factors

While the intrapersonal factors that students exhibited were a significant explanation for their ability to navigate their school environment, so too was the support they received from their family. For many students, close relationships with families and the strong cultural roots instilled in them by family were insulating factors against ROC. Sometimes this support came in the form of encouraging students to step out of the norm of what was expected of them. For example, it was Rita's mother who encouraged her attend the elite, predominantly white, public magnet high school she mentioned earlier:

> My mama, she was like, "Oh, I want you to go to [the magnet school]. . . . I was like, "I don't know what you are talking about, Mama." She was like, "No, you are going there." She made me fill out all the forms and printed it all out. We went to the little meetings. And she was like, "Yeah, I want you to go there." And I was like, "Ok, Mama."

The exchange with her mother that Rita recounted was heartwarming. Her mother was firm with her expectations and belief that Rita could be successful at the prestigious magnet school. Without her mother's encouragement, Rita would probably not have applied for admission. Rita did not suggest that any of her teachers or other school personnel talked with her about the opportunity to attend a different school. Rather, it was Rita's mother who saw what was possible for Rita before she could see it for herself.

Rita's mother encouraged her to apply to a magnet school. Other families provided their children with more general support, but support that was just as critical to their success. For example, families often offered important advice about how to navigate the racism students would inevitably experience. To this point, Adriana talked about how her parents' lessons were critical to her success. Her parents explained to her at a young age that because they paid tuition for her to attend a private parochial school, her teachers had to treat her well:

> [My parents] taught me to really be aggressive. Another thing was I was in the private school and they always had to pay, and they were like, "We are paying them." You know? So, I never let anyone yell at me, as far as like the teachers and the administration. I was like, "No, I am sorry." I had this one math teacher who was always yelling, and I was just like, "I'm sorry, are you yelling at me? I need you to repeat that." Because I was not going to get yelled at because I [was paying] $6,000 to be sitting in that classroom. That was important for me. I always knew what was right, and I told them.

I appreciated what Adriana's parents taught her, that no teacher had the right to yell at her and should be explaining the lesson in a way her young mind could understand. Another aspect of teaching her to be aggressive included speaking up for herself, especially when it came to talking about her heritage. Continuing her conversation, Adriana shared this example from kindergarten:

> My teacher, she was like, "Tomorrow we're going to make Pilgrim hats." So I went home and told my mom. I was like, "Mom are we Pilgrims or Indians?" And she was like, "You're Indian and the white man stole your land and killed your people." I went to school, and the teacher said, "Ok everyone, get up and put on your Pilgrim hats!" And I said, "No! I'm an Indian and the white man stole my land and killed my people." I got sent to the principal's office, where I repeated it a couple of times 'cause they kept asking me why I was there. And they called my mother. She was like, "Well, it's true. The white man stole our land and killed our people." I was taught to tell the truth. I was taught that I paid you so you [will] not yell at me and you will not put me down.

Although Adriana's family was not wealthy, they helped her understand in a straightforward manner that her teachers should not treat her badly. A complementary lesson to that was that she should stand up for herself even if it meant disagreeing with her teachers. She should be respectful, but that did not mean she had to let teachers yell at her. This may seem like a small point, but given the number of microaggressions these students experienced from teachers and other adults (for example, the teacher who laughed when Emma shared her dream of attending Harvard), the knowledge that she had permission from her parents to speak up in the face of injustice was powerful for Adriana. In contrast, I was reminded about what Rick said in the focus group about trusting what his teachers said:

> [I]n the position as a student, you think the higher-ups are right, in a sense. So, I mean, why am I gonna oppose a teacher who's been here fifteen years? Obviously, he has some legitimacy to what he's saying.

Many of the students felt as Rick did and were taught to trust what their teachers told them. Thus, the message Adriana received from her parents at an early age, that she should speak up for herself and that adults were not always right, was powerful in helping her build confidence. It allowed her to work through negative experiences with teachers that may have caused others to stumble. This point about teachers being an obstacle for some students is complex, as they were also an important source of support for many students. However, by helping Adriana know that her teachers might not always be right, her parents helped her be better able to brush off or explicitly counter the negative messages her teachers may have sent her way. Further, if Adriana were ever called out for her behavior, she knew that her parents would have her back.

One of the ROCs students experienced was a distancing from family. This was another complicated finding because even as students navigated strained relationships with various family members, they also credited their family with giving them the skills that helped them be successful. This is demonstrated by Adriana's and Rita's stories. Gregg spoke to this issue directly, talking about how though he felt some jealousy from some of his cousins, they were also incredibly supportive of him:

> You could tell there was a slight little bit of jealousy, but it was nothing to the point where it was, like, real tense situations. We grew up together and they knew that I was the one, and they always kind of

> told me, when they came down to being honest, like, "Man, you're gonna do everything that we were supposed to do." They were all really proud of me.

Gregg's words were touching as he talked about the support he received from his cousins. Although there was tension, I also sensed a bit of sadness when Gregg said his cousins "knew that [he] was the one." It was clear to them that he would be the one to make it, and they were proud and supportive of him for it. This is the tension that ROC picks up, that even as we are happy that these students have achieved academic success, the cost is not something that can be overlooked. Nor can the fact that so many other students are left behind in a system that makes achievement so difficult to attain when giving up or being distanced from the family and friends whom they love is necessary.

Mentors and mentoring program capacity factors

Given the complex school environments the students were navigating, perhaps it is not surprising that programs outside of the normal school structure had an important impact on their experiences. Thus, another important non-school factor pertinent to the ROC framework is the role of various mentoring programs. Several of the students we talked with credited relationships formed with mentors with helping them build the social and cultural capital necessary to sustain their academic success. For example, Northern College had a relationship with an organization called "Posse"—a program for high school students that trained small groups of students in leadership development to effect change on the college campuses they attended together. Several of the students we interviewed at Northern College came through the Posse Chicago program, though sometimes in different cohort years. Students mentioned the program in the course of talking about aspects of their environment that helped them be successful. Emma talked about the role Posse played in helping her overcome the challenge of leaving her family to go to college out of state:

> I remember I had to get myself together for the Posse and just toward the end [of the eight-month training] it was no longer about me, it was about the Posse. Just knowing that you had no other choice but to come here. Ready or not, you had to come. And I wasn't ready to

> say bye to my parents, I wasn't ready to [say goodbye to] family at all. My van drove off, and my little sister [was] yelling, "I love you!" And me just kind of being like really alone here. Like, walking away from the [central campus quad area] and seeing all the little families together. And how my family had to leave to get home on time 'cause work starts on Monday. And me yelling back at [my sister] when I realized she [had] yelled at me 'cause I was so zoned out. I was like, "I love you past the universe!" And that being the last words I told her. I yelled at her as she drove off. It's just, um, not having a choice. You are here. I had to be here. I had gotten Posse and so I wasn't here for myself, I was here for my Posse.

Emma was incredibly close with her family. She played an important caregiving role for her younger siblings, but she relied on her family for strength, too. Her discussion of the role Posse played in her life was meant to explain its importance in helping her remember that she also had a role to play with her group, that they supported each other. Without that deep support, it was unclear how she would have navigated the deep gulf between her life in Chicago and life at Northern College. As she said, she remained grounded in the fact that she was not there [just] for herself, but also for her Posse.

Adriana was also a Posse Scholar at Northern College. She had also participated in a different mentoring program in high school that focused on providing a variety of college information and mentoring to low-income students in the Chicago area. The skills she learned in that program compensated for the lack of information about going to college provided by her school, as she explained:

> [The program] provides you with academic help. Not only financially, but we had like mentors, like individual mentors in high school. We also had training sessions that we went to, like facilitation sessions. So, at a young age, like freshman in high school, I was already exposed to that and getting good grades and bumping up your GPA as a freshman. I had like a lot of guidance in high school. I think that's when I realized, like, "Oh, I have to take this seriously." My freshman year and sophomore year, we were already talking about colleges.

Adriana did not learn about going to college or how "getting good grades and bumping up your GPA" could be helpful in going to college or getting a scholarship from her high school. Rather, she learned about it from her mentors in this program. This provided Adriana with important information that fostered her success. However, her friends who were not in the program did not receive that information directly. Further, her participation in these programs made it more difficult for her to maintain relationships with her friends, as she was always headed off to meetings for one organization or the other, and they could not go with her.

Both Emma and Adriana talked about mentoring organizations that existed outside of their high schools, but some students attended schools that incorporated these kinds of programs within the existing school structure. Araceli had high praise for a program at her school called Facing History and Ourselves, which provided an opportunity for students to openly discuss issues of injustice from a global perspective:

> You get to learn about things that happen around the world that you never even knew existed. I mean, it just opens up your eyes to everything that's out there. In terms of doing something right, yeah, I do think that is helping out educational systems. Because [our city] is a place where civil rights was a big thing, you know? You still hear about people, the Black versus white kind of thing, you still hear about that. The thing that they do is like you get to talk to people from so many backgrounds that otherwise you would not come into contact with. Maybe 'cause you thought that they couldn't keep a conversation like that, you know? Then you find out that they have so many experiences behind them and you are like, "Wow, that's intense."

For Araceli, whose Mexican American heritage was central to her identity, Facing History and Ourselves provided an important pathway to talk about all kinds of issues, including her culture. However, as an observer, I did wonder about the program's central focus on the Holocaust, or the fact that she saw civil rights as something "you still hear about" as if it was not a contemporary issue. Araceli was correct in making the connection to her city as a cornerstone of the civil rights movement, but it did not seem that this was a foundational component of the program. Students thus learned about injustice as something that happened "far away" from both a geographic and temporal perspective. However, she was able to make some connections that were not made explicit by the white teachers who ran the program. Despite the fact that there was a critical mass of Latinx students in the school, most of the discussion focused on "the Black versus white kind of thing" and ignored relevant information about her cultural heritage. I share Araceli's story because she saw it as an important part of her experiences. However, while this was probably better than not addressing these issues at all, the school missed out on an opportunity to tie these larger issues in with the also-relevant racial injustices affecting their students and families.

The experiences Emma, Adriana, and Araceli shared here point to the importance of these mentoring programs. The people and programming helped mediate what may otherwise have been an insurmountable challenge. For Emma, the connections she had built with her Posse gave her something to focus on when she felt overwhelmed when her family dropped her off for college. Adriana learned important information about going to college and strategies that would better prepare her from the program she participated in. Finally, Araceli credited her school's involvement in Facing History and Ourselves with creating space she needed to learn about history and teach her peers about her own family's heritage and cultural traditions. While I do not want to dismiss the importance of these programs, they do come with some additional cautions.

First, as important as these programs were for the students who participated in them, I cannot help but think about the students who were not participants. How many students at Adriana's school missed out on information that could have helped them go to college because they were not invited to participate in the college readiness mentoring program? Could Emma have handled moving away from her family if she had not been a part of Posse? Would the stand-alone programs at Northern College have been enough to help her find her place? Araceli was able to make additional connections with her culture with Facing History and Ourselves, but did other students tune out because the messages did not resonate with them?

Another caution comes in relying on external organizations to do this work. Indeed, an undue reliance on external mentoring programs can compromise the sense of belonging and community that is so critical to fostering positive school cultures that reduce ROC. An important positive school factor is cultivating an environment where students and adults can have open and frank discussions about race and racism. This is not something that can or should just be farmed out to an outside organization. Doing so can undermine efforts to cultivate an open and welcoming climate *within* the school. External programs or organizations can supplement, but never supplant, what is offered by the school.

ROC CLOSING THOUGHTS

Across these capacity factors, the ROC framework provided important explanatory value to existing work on non-school factors in academic success by showing how they are linked with systemic factors at the school level. Without this larger contextual perspective, we are gaslighting students. We know that academic success is tied into students' compliance with racialized expectations, although these rules are often hidden and deeply imbedded into the fabric of the school environment. Yet, despite having this information about the realities Black and Latinx students face, we insist instead that if students were just more resilient, their parents cared more, or they were paired with a mentor, then they would be academically successful. Ultimately, this problematic perspective deflects attention away from the school and our responsibility as educators to create an environment that does not require students to be so gritty. Carla made this point more succinctly than I ever could, telling us:

> Who's really coming out to see what we really go through? Who's on the Board having those discussions, those conversations? I don't know. Are our voices even really being heard, or are we just faded into the background, kept quiet and shy? And who's supposed to be representing us? Do they really know us? Because I think that if we had a voice, maybe things would be a little different and we could be able to have things that we need to be successful. Students in the suburbs don't go through the same things as the students from the inner city. Students who don't have money to have enough food to eat throughout the day. You know what I mean? Or, students who struggle, you know, are afraid to even walk to school. You know? These [suburban] kids have their parents chauffer them to school and stuff. . . . They just had all these things shown to them. I feel like they had more time. . . . The teachers have more time to dedicate to the students, to teach them and not so much quieting the class down.

Carla puts in sharp relief the point that what happens in the school environment matters quite a lot in terms of the opportunities students have to be successful. Students in Carla's school were incredibly capable and smart. Indeed, from her perspective, they were much grittier and more resilient than the white suburban students who "had all these things shown to them." Yet, she still saw those suburban students as more successful despite the fact that their pathways were smoother and their profiles more aligned with the norms and traditions that fuel the white logics that permeate our educational system. In our study, while families and outside mentors were critical to fostering students' positive experiences, I reiterate the point that these influences cannot be separated from the school environment itself. That is, it would be wrong to say that a primary way to reduce ROC would be to retain the services of a mentoring organization with no other intervention. It is first and foremost the school's responsibility to foster an inclusive and supportive environment.

In this chapter, I have worked to show the various interpersonal, family, and outside organization factors that helped mediate the students' experiences, but also how these factors were inextricably linked to larger systemic processes. It is important to be clear about the influence of these larger factors, as so much of the existing work on non-cognitive variables—be that grit, resilience, or similar perspectives—seems to focus on these internal factors. In the end, however, even some who espoused the importance of grit seem to have made that connection. Returning to the article that I opened this chapter with, I was surprised to see one of the conclusions shared at its close:

> Data showed that spending a few hours each week in close proximity to a certain kind of teacher changed *something* about students' behavior. And that was what mattered. Somehow these teachers were able to convey deep messages—perhaps implicitly or even subliminally—about belonging, connection, ability, and opportunity. And somehow those messages had a profound impact on students' psychology, and thus on their behavior. The environment those teachers created in the classroom, and the messages that environment conveyed, motivated students to start making better decisions—to show up to class, to persevere longer at difficult tasks, and to deal more resiliently with the countless small-scale setbacks and frustrations that make up the typical student's school day.

Here, the author made the connection that a young person's ability to "deal more resiliently" with the challenges they face was tied to what happens in the classroom, to the connections that teachers can make to foster a sense of connection and belonging that featured so prominently in the success stories our students shared. Undoubtedly, resilience is an important characteristic for students to possess. It helps students better navigate their school environment. However, these skills are not an *alternative* to what we do in schools. We can and we must foster school environments that promote success by attending to school factors. That is the most important point. Then, as part of that larger effort, we can also help students build resilience. We can work to forge strong relationships with families based on mutual respect and care. We can build programs and partner with other organizations to bolster efforts to share with students the knowledge that will help them be successful. If we can do these things, then we have a chance at effecting meaningful change.

ROC Talk: The Exception That Proves the Rule

Dr. Glenn A. Chambers

A note from Terah Venzant Chambers: In full disclosure, I have been married to Glenn Chambers for nearly fifteen years, and he has been part of this journey from the time ROC was just a series of hopeful but disparate thoughts. I was thrilled when he agreed to write a ROC Talk because his experience differs so significantly from mine and also from so many of the students in the study. Glenn attended public schools in Houston with Black teachers who truly cared about him and his classmates and who provided a foundation of love and care that he and his classmates carried with them throughout their lifetimes. In this ROC Talk, we are inspired to think about the power of nurturing school environments for transformative change.

I'll never forget the look on my best friend's face when he was introduced to my fifth-grade teacher at my wedding reception. Initially, he thought my former teacher was a relative, or someone from the neighborhood, because everyone at the reception knew my teacher and was genuinely excited to see him. Almost fourteen years later, my friend still mentions this encounter. He even shared the story with his mother, who expressed joy that I was able to sustain a relationship with a former teacher for so long but also regret that her son was not as "lucky." I met my friend in graduate school. He often recalled the horror stories of being one of a few Black students throughout his K–12 experience and the ways in which he felt targeted by teachers and administrators in his wealthy, suburban Northeast school district. I never heard him say anything positive about school. He was a working-class Black kid, raised by a single mother who worked extremely hard to create opportunities for her child. Moving into an upper-class community, where her son would have access to a "better education," was an obvious choice. But my friend recalls being constantly reminded of who he was not or what he lacked materially. Teachers and administrators had very low expectations of what he could achieve based almost solely on his race and economic status. The last thing he would want to see was a teacher from his K–12 years, and here was my fifth-grade teacher catching up with family and friends at my wedding! How does that happen? I have tried to answer this question since my friend first raised it. The answer is not a simple one, but I will try in what follows to offer some insight.

For the past sixteen years, I have been a history professor at two large research universities. One school is located in the South, the other in the Midwest. I am a historian of the Modern Caribbean specializing in the former British colonies post-emancipation. My work engages the impact of immigration on national discourses on race, ethnicity, and citizenship in the Caribbean and Central America. This work has allowed me to travel throughout the United States, Canada, the United Kingdom, the Caribbean, and Central America. I have even had the opportunity to fulfill a life-long goal of traveling to West Africa. I often find myself reflecting on these experiences to determine how I got to this point. How did a kid from the part of town that most people dismissed as poor, drug and crime infested, and by extension unworthy of care get to be a full professor at a major university? Neither of my grandfathers finished high school but were able to support their families through manual labor jobs in the warehouses and oil refineries in the area. Both of my grandmothers finished high school, but for most of their lives worked at home raising their large families (and occasionally working for white people doing domestic work) before taking on jobs outside the home once their children grew older. My mother and father were high school graduates. Both enrolled in college, but for a host of reasons never finished. I was taught the importance of hard work and school. However, the idea that I could "make it" and become a professor was not a given.

As a professor, I encounter a wide range of students from all racial, ethnic, and class backgrounds with varying levels of preparation for college. What some of my students lack in preparation, they make up for it in confidence and work ethic. Others who are "academically prepared" can struggle with thinking critically and independently. Part of this is due to the "testing culture" that has developed in K–12 education over the years, in which high-stakes testing has shifted the focus away from critical thinking and analysis to getting the correct answer and meeting certain benchmarks. It has instilled a culture, I believe, among students in which having the "right answer," being in the "right classes," or having the "right credentials" on your resume have overshadowed the importance of learning and developing the whole person in higher education. Growing up in Houston, Texas, in the 1980s and 1990s (I started kindergarten in 1982), school (and learning in general) for me was none of these things. It was a way out. When I talk about a way out, this is not in the sense of the all too generalized way out of poverty or a bad family situation that has become cliché when discussing students from low-income or underserved communities. My childhood did not fit these clichés. The "way out" for me was a way out of limited thinking, a way out of limited options, and a way up to see the beauty of life, its possibilities, and where I fit into it all.

Despite my humble beginnings, I went on to earn a college degree. I was also the first to go to graduate school, earn a master's degree and PhD, and pursue a career in academia. My younger siblings also went on to earn college degrees and master's degrees and are gainfully employed. Several of my childhood friends also excelled in education and have gone on to lead very productive and fulfilling lives. How did we do it? How did we beat the odds? That five-year-old kindergartener could have never imagined the life he would live, the experiences he would have, the opportunities to travel the world, the various people he would encounter along the way. However, reflecting on my experiences, it becomes clear that the seeds for success were planted long ago and had everything to do with the community in which I was raised and my association with local public schools and its teachers. Although I could not have seen my potential at that time, there were countless teachers and administrators who did.

I was fortunate to attend an elementary school in which the principal, staff, and almost all of the teachers were African American, were educated at historically Black colleges and universities (HBCUs), and took very seriously the commitment to uplift the community through a holistic education. Many of the teachers lived (or had family) in the neighborhood, worshipped in the same local churches as their students, shopped in the same local establishments, and supported local youth educational and athletic programs. These were "race men and women" from an era in which the notion that the future of Black America depended on the educational success of its children. Not only did they believe this, but they were resigned to put that belief into practice in the classroom. Because my parents and their siblings had grown up in the same community in which my siblings and I were raised, some of my teachers in elementary school had also taught my parents, aunts, uncles, and other extended family. It was a *community school* in the truest sense of the term.

The curriculum in the school was fairly standard. We were, after all, in the Houston Independent School District, which was both one of the largest in the state and situated in one of the largest urban centers in the South. Looking back, the school was under-resourced and underfunded. However, what the school lacked in financial resources, it made up for in creativity and innovation. I often tell friends and colleagues who study race and the Black experience that I learned more about Black history from kindergarten through fifth grade than I did in all my years of college and graduate school. This is not to say that these latter experiences were not life-changing or did not play a significant role in my success. Rather, the point is that the tools I needed to be successful as an academic were taught to me as a very young child and provided a strong foundation on which to build. It was in elementary school that I first began to learn about Africa. It was also in elementary school that I first encountered conversations about slavery; Jim Crow; migration; jazz; blues; and historical Black figures, such as W. E. B. Du Bois, Harriet Tubman, Bill Pickett, Booker T. Washington, and others. My mother still has many of my elementary school book reports on various aspects of Black History that were assigned year-round (not just during Black History Month). We learned to sing "Lift Every Voice and Sing" at assemblies, and when an increasing number of Spanish-speaking students arrived in the school, we learned the Pledge of Allegiance in Spanish, too! Some of my fondest memories are the opportunities we had on Fridays: students would present their best work for the week to the principal, who would stamp the work with a ribbon and allow us to pick a piece of candy from her jar if we had done a good job (she always had the *best* candy!). There was also mandated library time in which we were taught the Dewey Decimal System, how to use the card catalogue, and where the public libraries were in the area (this proved especially important for me later on).

While it is easy to be nostalgic about the fond memories of my early education, I would be remiss to avoid some of the issues. I recall one experience in second grade in which the class was given spelling books for the semester. Each student received a used book, which was common (occasionally new textbooks were distributed, depending on the grade level or curriculum changes). When I opened my book to write my name in it as instructed, I noticed that a previous user of the book was my aunt, who was ten years older than me. There were even other names listed before hers. This was clear evidence that the school had not received new spelling books in over ten years! I experienced something similar with a math book in fourth grade: I was assigned a book that an aunt who was twelve years older than me had used previously. Despite the age of the books, I still learned how to spell and do math. However, I mention this only to demonstrate that the school was by no means without struggles. What we lacked in resources was made up for in love from the teachers and the principal and the confidence they instilled in their students. When I went to school, I felt like it was an extension of home. The teachers were an extension of my parents, grandparents, great-aunts and great-uncles, and all the elders in the community whom I respected and admired.

In sixth grade, I was accepted into a pre-International Baccalaureate (IB) program at a middle school. The school was on the north side of the town where I grew up but was located in a predominantly white neighborhood. Houston was notoriously segregated at the time and I had very limited interactions with whites on any level prior to middle school. I was bused to school, but so were many of the other kids, regardless of race or economic background. The honors programs drew students from across the city and was extremely diverse. However, the teachers were overwhelmingly white, as were the principal and office staff. When I arrived at the school, I was excited about learning and the new possibilities. Other kids from my neighborhood also went to the school, so I had a built-in network of friends to make the transition relatively smooth. However, I did find it odd that there were few Black teachers at the school, and they *all* knew who I was! This was a different neighborhood, a new school, a new experience entirely. I had never seen any of these teachers before. How did they know me? I found out years later that my Black teachers from elementary school were college classmates of many of the Black teachers in middle school, and later high school. In fact, it was my fifth-grade teacher who had recommended to my parents that I apply to the pre-IB program at that particular middle school in the first place. They were keeping up with me! They were making sure that I was okay! I was being tracked! Not in the "in-school segregation" way, but in a way that proved much more valuable. These teachers saw potential in me and wanted to make sure that I was successful.

As I progressed through middle school and entered high school, I continued to grow as a student. It seemed as if white teachers cared less, and their expectations, even in the IB classes, were different for Black and Brown students than they were for white students. Many of the teachers had attended the major flagship universities in the state (as had the parents of many of my white classmates) and were engrossed in various degrees of "white Texas culture" at the time. I always felt that this was at odds with who I was and what I believed as a Black person. No one was openly malicious or racist toward me. Teachers didn't discourage me in the ways that my friend from graduate school experienced. However, they did not necessarily encourage me, either. School ceased to feel like an extension of home and the community, and the curriculum reflected the experiences of my white peers more than my own.

I saw many of my Black and Brown peers become alienated by this. Some started acting out in class or focused solely on sports, to the detriment of their grades. Others fell into drugs (this was the crack era) and alcohol, teen pregnancy, and all of the other clichés. This is not to say that some of the paths my peers took were because of the school. Life happens. There are as many positive stories as there are negative stories from my K–12 years. My point is that when school became a less welcoming place, I leaned on the foundation established by my Black teachers in elementary school and found a saving grace in the library and the positive examples in my community. I had confidence. I knew I could learn. More importantly, I knew where the information was and how to access it. Just because someone said something didn't make it true! I have countless bus fare and later gas receipts of the numerous evenings and weekends that I spent in high school going to the various branches of the Houston Public Library just because I wanted to know things, or because I did not believe all of the Eurocentric curriculum that I was forced to learn (and be tested on). Also, because my foundation for what constituted a good teacher was based on those early experiences, whenever I experienced a teacher later on in my studies whose approach ran counter to that, I never internalized it.

I'm certain that not everyone I grew up with had the same experiences that I did. Not everyone in my community was able to attain the same level of education or have the types of experiences that have defined my professional career. Also, most of us went to different middle schools and high schools. Some of us were tracked into honors programs, and others were relegated to underfunded and under-resourced schools. However, when I reminisce with old friends from the neighborhood, most agree that despite the choices that people made or the situations that led to the diverging paths that some of us took, there was a period in elementary school when we all felt that we could do and be anything. That confidence can be attributed to none other than those teachers who made our success their primary mission. For them, I am forever grateful.

Terah Venzant Chambers's Take

When Glenn and I first discussed his writing a ROC Talk, he expressed concern that his experience was so different that it might stand out too much from the rest of the book. To me, his experiences provided an important counternarrative; they were exactly the reason why I knew they *needed* to be included. There are a few pieces related to the ROC framework that I would like to highlight from his story. First is the role of school factors. The standout in his experience is the foundation he received during his elementary years. His teachers were overwhelmingly Black, well-educated, and deeply committed to the Houston neighborhood in which they worked. It is so important to make this distinction because too often "underfunded" school becomes synonymous with "poor educational environment." This could not be further from the truth. Historically, Black segregated schools were significantly under-resourced. Monetary and other material resources were systematically and nearly exclusively diverted to white schools.[1]

Nonetheless, historians of education like Dr. Vanessa Siddle Walker have documented the ways these "under-resourced" schools offered an opportunity much like the one Glenn discussed, where teachers were nevertheless highly qualified and deeply dedicated to their craft and to their students.[2] In Glenn's experience, teachers were purposeful in exposing students to Black history—all the time, not just during Black History Month. They also practiced culturally responsive pedagogy, incorporating opportunities for students to learn Spanish when the demographics of the school began to shift, bringing more Mexican American families to the school. Glenn also reported that his Black teachers continued to keep tabs on him even after he left the elementary school. I can imagine they were also purposeful in cultivating the network of Black students into the pre-IB program he referenced and making sure that the Black teachers at his middle school continued to have him and his friends on their radar and continued to look out for them. Thus, although he entered a predominantly white school space for the first time, in middle school he benefited from the continued thought and care established by his Black elementary teachers.

Glenn will tell you that he did not really personally identify with the idea of racial opportunity cost. Still, he could see the ways in which the framework explains the pathways that his friend from graduate school or I traveled. Even attending a predominantly white college, he was keen to replicate the Black community that he was accustomed to from his earliest ages. Probably without conscious thought, Glenn replicated the care he was used to from elementary school in the community of Black peers and colleagues on campus. So, I disagree with Glenn. Far from negating the ROC framework, his story emphasizes its importance. I am thrilled to be able to include his narrative here, to showcase what we are trying to build: why cultivating a racially diverse teaching force is critically important and how a welcoming and caring climate can create a foundation for a lifetime of success.

Conclusion

> "I was team teaching in this program, and my colleagues were White," recalled [Dr.] View. "And there was a colleague who invited us to present to his class. And he said, 'This is Dr. So-and-so, and this is Dr. So-and-so, and then he just sort of looked at me and said, 'And this is Jenice.' And I said, 'No, it's Dr. View.' He knew damn good and well that that was true. But it seemed important to him to present me as less-than. That was maybe, in the academy, one of the most in-my-face expressions of 'You don't belong.' But, you know, there are countless others."[1]

The quote above is from an *Edutopia* article that a colleague posted on her social media feed. The article, "Why Black Teachers Walk Away," highlighted findings from an empirical research study that connected Black teachers' experiences with racism with their decision to leave the teaching profession. In the article, coauthor Dr. View shared her own experience as a Black university professor, including the racial microaggressions that sent her the message that she did not belong—what I interpreted as the racial opportunity cost she bore as a result of navigating racial norms present in higher education. I have always known that the white logics that the students in my project encountered were the same faced by other racially minoritized populations, such as higher education faculty like Dr. View or the Black K–12 teachers who were the focus of her and her colleagues' research. I start with this vignette because it helps concretize the ways in which the racial opportunity cost (ROC) framework might be used in expanded ways compared to how it has been presented thus far, or the "forward-leading" aspects of this work.

In each chapter of this book I have focused on deeply elucidating various elements of the ROC framework at a granular level. I was intentional about starting with the school and how aspects of the culture (school factors) were reflective of white racial logics that set up expectations that Black and Latinx students were meant to follow if they wanted to be seen as academically successful. I then spelled out clearly the impact on the Black and Latinx students who had to navigate these expectations—the racial opportunity cost that resulted from their school environment—as well as the role of other aspects of their social identities (intersectional factors) and other non-school elements (capacity factors). However, I have not yet discussed how these various aspects of the ROC framework work together from a macro perspective. In addition, while I have clearly identified the mechanisms within schools that can increase the ROC that Black and Latinx students experience, I have not specifically addressed the actions educators must take to alleviate racial opportunity cost. The purpose of this chapter, then, is threefold. First, I will highlight the synergistic aspects of the ROC framework through an example provided by a close examination of three focal students. Second, I will offer recommendations for action for educators who want to apply the ROC framework to their local context to reduce racial opportunity cost. Finally, I will talk about the broader applications of the ROC framework to additional contexts, including higher education and other populations (such as Black and Latinx teachers or school leaders).

ROC FRAMEWORK: PUTTING IT ALL TOGETHER

Each of the previous chapters has offered an opportunity to fully explicate the details of various aspects of the ROC framework. Providing these more detailed analyses in separate chapters allowed for the deep engagement of relevant issues; however, the downside was that the interaction of these factors, a critical aspect in fully understanding what the students experienced, may have been minimized. Accordingly, I will address the interrelated nature of aspects of the ROC framework through the experiences of three focal students. This exercise will allow me to more fully examine the ways in which school factors, intersectional factors, and capacity factors worked together to promote or alleviate the racial opportunity cost that the students experienced. It will also foster a better understanding of how each element of the ROC framework is part of the whole, where what happens with one impacts the rest.

Choosing just three students to highlight was difficult: while much has been shared about each one's experiences, there is, of course, even more that is relevant to their stories and the racial opportunity cost they incurred that has not been discussed. For example, there was so much more to say in Gregg's story about gender expectations, the broader context of his neighborhood, and his own sense of determination. Similarly, Araceli's family support helped color her experiences in beautiful and powerful ways, and I wished for the space to highlight those elements of her story. In the end, I chose to focus on Micayla, Rick, and Emma because while their stories have a lot in common, there are also differences that are useful in highlighting the synergistic elements of the ROC framework. I will not review *all* of the school factors, intersectional factors, and capacity factors introduced in this book, but rather emphasize a select few in service to this larger point.

Micayla

When I think about the whole of Micayla's experiences and the racial opportunity cost she experienced, I am struck most by the significant interplay between her school environment (school factors) and the preparation and support she received from her family (capacity factors). Recall that Micayla attended one of the most elite public high schools in Texas in an area of the city inhabited by the most affluent citizens. Because of the school's location, it also had a fairly diverse student body. To have a chance at enticing white, affluent families to keep their children enrolled in public school (and not opt for private school), school leaders, according to Micayla, had basically created a "school within a school," where most of the rich kids and the small number of racially minoritized students who "fit the mold" academically were enrolled in the prestigious international baccalaureate (IB) program (school factor: structural). From my perspective, it was also fairly clear that the school had established performative expectations for students. These expectations were revealed in the stories Micayla shared; for example, always being careful about how she spoke in class after her white classmates once ridiculed her when she spoke in African American Vernacular English (racial opportunity cost: representation cost). However, when we asked her directly if enrolling in advanced classes ever made her feel that she had to change the way she presented herself, she pushed back, referring to how close she was with other Black students who were not in her classes and the pride she carried for her racial heritage. Micayla vehemently rejected the idea that she needed to cater to these expectations in order to be successful. This pushback provides an important opportunity to examine what her response tells us about the racial opportunity cost that she experienced.

Micayla's insistence that she never had to change in order to fit in stood in contrast to her reports of adjusting her language in the face of daily scrutiny. How do we make sense of Micayla's response with the contrary evidence she provided? Did she simply lack awareness of what was happening? It was not that she did not understand the reality of the situation. I believe her response reflected her struggle to reconcile the reality of her situation with her core beliefs. Clearly, the two positions were in deep tension with one another. This struggle is reflective of what I term racialized identity dissonance (racial opportunity cost: psychosocial costs). As a racial opportunity cost, racialized identity dissonance reflected the struggle some students had in trying to make sense of their identity as "smart" Black and Latinx students in light of the larger institutionalized racial dynamics they navigated. Racialized identity dissonance explained Micayla's pushback against our question because while the racialized expectations present in her school had real consequences for her as a Black student, she fundamentally resented the idea that she would have to change her behavior in deference to them—even though she told us that she did just that. Given how important her racial identity was to her, Micayla seemed uncomfortable with the idea that she *should* have to do this, much like other students who expressed similar perspectives about their situations. In concert with the racial opportunity cost framework, the concept of racialized identity dissonance stands as an important contribution to our understanding of racially minoritized students' experiences in white-normed school spaces. Traditional explanations have cast this tension as originating within the students themselves, suggesting that they fear being seen as "acting white" and thus eschew achievement.[2] However, racialized identity dissonance as a manifestation of the racial opportunity cost some students incurred properly contextualized this struggle as a result of the white racial logics with which they were constantly forced to contend.

But what helped Micayla persevere through the challenges she faced, even as she experienced significant racial opportunity cost? Without a doubt, both capacity factors and intersectional factors were important to understand as mediating factors in her experience. First and foremost, in terms of capacity factors, Micayla deserved credit for her success. Her strong sense of self-determination even in the face of significant challenges was a critical factor. In addition, Micayla's family was also instrumental in helping her buffer the challenges she faced in school. They had instilled in her a strong sense of racial pride. She recalled having conversations with them during dinner where they learned about Black history and discussed current events. It was clear that this foundation helped insulate her from the racialized expectations she faced at school and allowed her to find community with other Black students. This grounding also helped her to not let the fact that she was one of few black students in IB classes lead her to question whether she belonged or was smart enough. She needed that sense of community in the moments where she did feel targeted, when her white classmates teased her for speaking Black English.

Micayla's family played an important role in terms of intersectionality factors, as well. Of all the students in our project, Micayla came from a relatively more affluent background. Although her self-reported social class was "middle class" (and that likely felt right to her, given the extreme wealth of many of her classmates), Micayla's mom was a college professor and her dad a lawyer; both had advanced degrees. Their social and cultural capital, which aligned with the dominant norms present and valued in her school, provided an additional advantage for Micayla as she worked to navigate her school's racialized expectations. It did not eliminate the challenge, to be sure, but it created a path that was less fraught than the path faced by Rick, or certainly Emma.

Rick

Rick and Micayla had similar high school experiences despite his attending a private Jesuit college preparatory high school and Micayla a traditional public school. Both students experienced elite, predominantly white educational environments: Rick's was a result of a selective recruiting and admissions process, Micayla's was due to the creation of a separate IB program that catered to wealthy white families. Thus, structural factors, specifically tracking, were more impactful in Micayla's experience. Further, Micayla felt that at her school, once students were accepted into the IB program and kept up strong grades, they had greater freedom of expression. Rick's school had more explicit rules for dress and conduct (school factor: climate factors). His wearing a uniform every day was just one example, but he shared numerous stories about the ways in which his school's expectations for speech, behavior, and dress were ever present. In addition, Rick struggled to maintain meaningful connections with other racially minoritized students; as a result, teachers became his friends. His positive relationships with teachers, school leaders, and other school personnel were a source of pride for him. His face lit up in his conversation with us when he recalled bringing teachers gifts and the special relationship he had formed with many of them (school factor: relationship factors).

However, Rick's recollections about the positive relationships he had with his teachers highlighted the dual nature of many aspects of the ROC framework; in his case, the strong connection he formed with teachers and the protective element that it offered also contributed to the racial opportunity cost that he experienced. His teachers and school leaders often leaned on him to be an ambassador for diversity, calling on him to take visitors on tours and generally embody the role of a "successful" racially minoritized student (racial opportunity cost: representation cost). Rick felt proud to serve in this capacity . However, Rick's teachers calling on him to be an exemplar for what their racially minoritized students could achieve was not only deeply problematic, but also ironic, given the overwhelming loneliness and isolation he reported feeling throughout high school (racial opportunity cost: psychosocial cost). Although these are separate racial opportunity costs, when taken as a whole, the mutually reinforcing nature of these experiences offer an additional lens through which to understand Rick's story.

Despite the challenges he faced at his school and the ROC he experienced, Rick was able to achieve success. How? The explanations are both similar to and different from Micayla's. Both students share in their capacity factors the sense of inner strength or fortitude that allowed them to be successful. Indeed, all of the students we talked to possessed a discernable inner strength and sense of resilience. From there, though, Micayla and Rick's paths diverge fairly significantly. In terms of other capacity factors, while Rick certainly had support from his family, he did not have that same buffer of racial pride that Micayla's parents had instilled in her, presumably from having navigated similar consequences of white logics in their own educational and professional careers. Rick's family loved and cared for him, too, that was obvious. His father was a high school principal and remained active in his life even when he and Rick's mother were no longer a couple. As noted above, one skill Rick cultivated was an ability to foster positive relationships with the adults around him. He had mastered the art of reading social and environmental cues. Even during his interview with us, Rick was keenly attentive to the questions we asked but also quick to offer some of his own about the broader purpose of our research. He came across to me as a person who was used to assessing a situation and quickly gaining a sense of what the implicit rules were, skills that certainly assisted him in successfully navigating high school and college despite not having the same social and cultural capital as Micayla.

However, while some students reported having a love for culture almost insistently poured into them (think Araceli or Micayla), this was not Rick's experience. In fact, navigating this aspect of his identity created somewhat of a challenge for him. While Rick was proud of his heritage, those around him seemed only to acknowledge his Black identity despite his growing up in what he described as a Puerto Rican household with his mother and grandmother. This tension over not having his Puerto Rican heritage recognized and validated was a point he shared with Emma, who similarly struggled to have her preferred identity acknowledged.

Emma

Emma provided a rich case study, as her experience was different from not only Rick and Micayla, but also from many of the other students in the project. One reason for that was the undeniable strength of personality that radiated from her soul that was unmatched by any of the other students with whom we spoke. This says a lot, as each of the students was magnetic in their own way. Another reason she stood out was because the high school she attended was significantly different from many of the others. It was an urban high school, not unlike the schools that Rick and Micayla attended; all were located in a large metropolitan area. However, what stood out about Emma's high school was that it was a typical, traditional high school that had suffered from years of underfunding and systemic neglect of the resources that an effective learning environment requires. Despite her taking many honors and advanced placement classes, Emma felt that her high school did not prepare her well for college. (Syril shared a similar story about his high school preparation in Texas, telling us that although advanced placement courses were offered, students who took the AP exams rarely scored above a 1 or 2, the lowest possible scores). Emma's assessment of her school's poor preparation is supported by a look at her school's ranking on the *U.S. News and World Report* "College Readiness Index," which awarded the school a 20 out of 100 rating.[3]

Unlike Emma, Rick and Micayla experienced an elite educational environment that had high expectations for academic success and provided the resources necessary for students to excel. Importantly, these elite programs were offered to only a select, predominantly white, minority relative to their schools' broader demographics. Rick's private school had strict admissions criteria that racially minoritized students who matriculated from the city's public school system likely struggled to meet. Micayla's high school practiced opportunity hoarding, ensuring that only those students who participated in its prized IB program were rigorously prepared for college. Micayla told us that the broader, more racially diverse population of students in the school was largely ignored.[4] Emma's experience makes her stand out because her school did not offer a rigorous academic pathway that would prepare her to attend one of the most elite colleges in the nation.[5] However, because her story stands out, it is important to unpack what the experience meant for her and the ROC she incurred.

One critically important point to highlight from Emma's experience, and one of the reasons I selected her as a focal student, had to do with the overall culture present in her school. Throughout this book, I have emphasized that white racial logics permeate our educational spaces and dictate rules for academic success regardless of local demographics. This may be hard to believe of a school like Emma's, where today the school is approximately 66 percent Latinx and 33 percent Black, with 94 percent of students qualifying for free or reduced-price lunch (and with several teachers from racially minoritized backgrounds, if a review of the teacher pages on the school website is a reliable gauge). However, Emma revealed several indicators that let us know that those white-normed expectations were alive and well in her school, too. For example, Emma shared that her identities of being "Latina" and "smart" were seen as being in conflict with one another, and that her classmates could not make sense of those identities together (school factor: climate factor). Even at this school, where most of the students were from racially minoritized backgrounds, they were still inculcated with the societal message that academic success was associated with whiteness. Importantly, connecting to points made earlier, the specific racial demographics of the school did not absolve it from being caught up in the same white logics that were present across all of the schools our participants attended.

Navigating these expectations was what set Emma up for the racial opportunity costs she experienced. Not surprisingly, like Rick, Emma was held up as the model of success by her teachers. However, while for Rick this seemed to be more about proving that there were racially minoritized students who excelled in the elite school, almost to prove that they were not racist, Emma carried the weight of a different sort of expectation. In this under-resourced school, where a small set of dedicated and committed teachers tried to persevere against the tide of other less qualified and committed teachers and a general lack of necessary resources, Emma was lifted up as a hope for what students could achieve (racial opportunity cost: representation cost). Emma was "proof" that in the larger bureaucratic network of public schools, theirs should not be written off. Of course, just as it was not fair for Rick's teachers to put this burden on him, it was unfair for Emma to be portrayed in this manner. For one thing, it created tension with her peers and family (racial opportunity cost: community cost); she had to tread lightly with her classmates, only to discover that her teachers were sabotaging her efforts behind the scenes by singling her out as what they should aspire to achieve.

So, what can help us make sense of Emma's success? What allowed her to persevere through circumstances that even in our sample of students stood out as particularly daunting? Capacity factors emerged as a particularly important consideration. Without a doubt, Emma's personality played a role. In fact, our understanding of those internal factors, that sense of inner strength or resilience that many students in our project displayed, crystallized after Emma's interview. We could not help but marvel at the significance of her sheer determination to be successful, and it caused us to reflect on our conversations with other students and make that connection. At the same time, we knew that her sheer will, though incredible, was likely inadequate on its own to explain her success. Despite all odds, her path led her to attend Northern College, something no one else in her family or her school had done. However, the strength of her personality and strong will were not the sole determinant of her success.

What also stands out about Emma's experience in addition to her resilience and inner-strength is the influence of another capacity factor that did not emerge significantly in either Rick nor Micayla's experiences: the influence of an external mentoring group. It was Emma's involvement in a third-party leadership organization that she credited with helping her go away for college. The leadership skills she gained there as well as the social and cultural capital she amassed were instrumental in how her story turned out. Emma even told us that it was her devotion to and responsibility toward her peers that explained how she was able to physically leave her home to drive to the campus with her family. Ultimately, despite her fears, she did not want to let her peers down. She had that sense of resilience and inner strength, the importance of which cannot be discounted. However, many kids have that same drive and are not able to overcome the challenge of attending a school that did not prepare them well. This is another reason Emma's story provides a compelling case study of the role of capacity factors. They explain how she was able to achieve success, but also their limitation in providing a systemic solution. Emma succeeded in spite of her school environment, not because of it. Ultimately, her story highlights the point made earlier about the danger of relying on capacity factors as a solution because this focus alone could not help other students at Emma's school. Not everyone could be accommodated in the leadership program in which she participated. Emma's story serves as a reminder of the importance of providing high-quality instructional resources to all schools, a point I will return to later in this chapter.

A closer examination of Micayla's, Rick's, and Emma's stories helped provide a deeper understanding of how their school environments combined with capacity and intersectionality factors to influence their experiences. However, while looking at intersectional and capacity factors provided this fuller picture, what should emerge from this analysis is knowledge of the absolute dominance of school factors and the challenge presented by the broader systemic issues present in schools. This closer examination confirmed that although the focus in this book was on Black and Latinx students who had been academically successful, the real contribution was about the larger educational apparatus. Seeing the ways in which the students in this project persevered and the racial opportunity cost they experienced along the way says much more about the system than it does about their own journeys. This is not about their status as high-achieving students, but what we can learn from their stories about the larger structures that undergird our educational system. Through their stories, we better understand the experiences of other racially minoritized students who have not achieved the same measure of success.

The truth is, racially minoritized students attending Rick's or Micayla's school would not likely have fared any better than students at Emma's school. Rick reported that few racially minoritized students were admitted to his private school; many who did were academically neglected and did not do well. And Micayla was quite forthcoming in telling us that most of the racially minoritized students who attended her public school were completely ignored in favor of the IB students, who received a disproportionate amount of the academic resources in the school. Again, the students' stories in this book highlight the ways we are institutionally failing most Black and Latinx students, regardless of whether they attend an elite private school in the suburbs or a traditional public school in the city.

RECOMMENDATIONS FOR ACTION: EFFECTING CHANGE BY ADDRESSING SCHOOL FACTORS

While the students' stories highlight the magnitude and importance of the systemic challenges we face in our educational system, they should also inspire our commitment to change. We may not be able to solve systemic racism, but there remains much that we can do to make an appreciable difference for Black and Latinx students who matriculate in our schools. In this section, I will address the ways in which educators in the participants' schools could have intervened. I will also speak more generally about recommendations for action that cut across the students' experiences. Without a doubt, our greatest opportunity to cultivate the kinds of school environments that reduce racial opportunity cost and improve students' experiences is through school factors, those aspects within a school environment that reflect broader societal values. These are the institutionalized processes that guide so much of what we do in schools, but that we are taught not to see. How do we work to interrupt or dismantle these school factors? I will first outline a few general responses and then directly address the three categories of school factors (climate factors, structural factors, and relationship factors).

The first point is that there are no quick fixes. At least, there are no quick fixes that are not accompanied by longer-term strategies for change. In the short term, there could very well be interventions that can be implemented fairly easily once a problem is noted, like eliminating a social studies assignment that is found to be racially problematic. On its face, this is a relatively simple intervention. However, this kind of response is never the *only* answer. Other questions must be asked, as well. How did the social studies assignment become part of the curriculum in the first place? Is a broader review of the social studies curriculum warranted to flag other potentially concerning assignments? What about other subjects? And what steps should be in place to proactively prevent something like this from happening? Who reviews the curriculum, and is there a diverse stakeholder group involved in that process? Are they sufficiently trained to make diversity, equity, and inclusion (DEI)-informed curricular choices? Who made the decision to give students the assignment? Is broader learning needed to help teachers fully understand why the assignment was inappropriate? What harm was done to students who participated in this assignment, and how must we begin to address the damage done to our climate? When these kinds of situations occur, responding immediately is important, but so is stepping back to understand what a specific incident reveals about our broader climate. Because we are working against deeply engrained, systemic processes, it will take time to shift the culture. Even then, it will take continuous attention and thoughtful action to effect long-term change (and we will never, ever be "free" of racism).

The second point is that we must be prepared to do multiple things at once. This does not mean educators should not try to focus on doing things well, or that it is necessary to take on *everything* at once. It does mean that the change we take on often has two sides. We must work for small wins even as we are engaged in long-term culture shifts. We must search for systemic responses but be attentive to individual actions. We must be committed to action, but also to our continued learning and understanding. Most of all, we must remember that progress on these kinds of issues is not linear. It will often feel like we take two steps forward and then another step back. Enacting this type of change is an inherently iterative process, meaning that as we learn more, we are inspired to take action, which then often only reveals the larger scope of the work ahead and the need for deeper learning. This is why racial equity work must be understood as an effort of continual progress, not a time-bound effort. This is also another reason to think about measuring progress over time. It is an important point for accountability and transparency, but also for morale, as the work can be deeply exhausting when it is done with fidelity and authenticity. This is especially true when incidents occur that seem to undermine all of the progress made. However, we must remember that it is all part of the process.

The third point is to start with taking responsibility and not to discount our own expertise. I talk with many school leaders whose initial inclination when faced with a racial equity issue is to hire an external consultant to come in and "fix" the "problem." My response to these requests is usually twofold. First, I ask what work the school and/or district is willing to do themselves. What responsibility are they willing to accept regarding the systemic nature of the challenges they (we) face? Too often, our posture comes from a place of locating the issue with the student or their family instead of with ourselves and our own culpability. That is a tried and failed approach—for good reason. There is no room in racial equity work for approaches that are not accompanied by individual and collective responsibility. Second, people who feel very novice in their understanding of racial equity work are often experts regarding their contexts. Having that community-informed perspective is one of the most valuable contributions that an educator can offer. It is often the perspective that I most rely upon when working with schools and districts where I am not familiar with the local context. As every educator knows, there is what one learns in a teacher or leadership preparation program or in an internship placement, but that training can feel inadequate for the actual school context in which one finds themselves. Of course, the same is true with racial equity work. So, even if a school leader brings in a consultant to help with their team's journey, they must also understand that in order for that work to be effective, it must include meaningful partnerships with various school and community stakeholders. These groups must build on what is already known about the school and community context as they approach a deep examination of the school environment.

Having provided some overall framing thoughts for educators who are interested in making substantive change in their school contexts, I will now address some specific issues related to each of the school factors categories: climate factors, structural factors, and relationship factors. Remember, **climate factors** address the overall culture or environment that is cultivated in a school. For example, Ice shared with us that in his school, it was better to aspire to be a doctor or a lawyer than a mechanic. Rick shared that a series of racist incidents were swept under the rug rather than substantively addressed. Both of these are examples of school environments where the climate was very restrictive and white racial logics were strongly ingrained. The question is, what do we do about it? Across all three school factors, the first step is awareness, cultivating an environment where issues of race and racism and the presence of these racial logics can be noted and understood. With that awareness comes the opportunity to make change; however, the change can be complicated because, as noted above, substantively shifting school culture is a long-term, continuous endeavor. As a first step, interrupting the pattern of white logics requires working to shift the demographics of the school's teaching and leadership to reflect the student and community population. Relatedly, we must provide sustained and substantive professional learning about anti-racism and equity for existing staff. After all, the world we live in contains a range of diversity, so it is just as or even more important for students who come from racially homogenous white communities to gain exposure to educators from racially minoritized backgrounds and white educators who are committed to anti-racism. However, in addition to initiating targeted hiring, school leaders need to take steps to ensure that a more racially diverse staff is fully welcomed and that staff members will not be walking into an environment where they too are expected to conform to racialized performance expectations.

Both of the student examples highlighted the need for immediate change but also the deeper climate issue that lay underneath. For Ice, the immediate issue was his being told he should not want to be a mechanic. So, yes, school leaders should take measures to find out if there are people explicitly conveying such messages (and stop them); however, they must also look holistically at the school environment to determine how and where those messages are being transmitted. Similarly, school leaders in Rick's school should have discussed openly the racist incidents that occurred, and the perpetrator should have been appropriately disciplined. However, they also needed to develop clear policies about the consequences of these actions and taken steps to educate staff about these issues as part of a long-term professional learning endeavor.

Structural factors attend to places where we create separation through tracking or any other mechanism that results in inappropriate stratification. Micayla shared with us how her school created a school within a school where racially minoritized students outside of the IB program were basically ignored, receiving an education that was much lower in quality. Carla shared how her taking advanced classes made her feel that she was leaving her friends behind. These are examples of structural factors. While tracking and ability grouping are incorporated in this category, I also include ways in which students are systematically excluded from opportunity. Thus, structural factors could include policies related to special, alternative, and/or gifted education placements, disciplinary practices, etc. Given the mountain of evidence that suggests that tracking is not effective as well as our understanding of the ways in which these structural factors begin at early ages (think again back to Hatt's kindergarten work) but accumulate and are exacerbated over time, we can begin to see the magnitude of the issue.[6]

So, what should the leaders at Micayla's school have done? Contrary to how it might seem, tracking itself was not the problem—the problem was the system of institutionalized racism from which racialized tracking emerges. All children deserve access to high-quality instruction, and it is particularly important at young ages. When students reach high school, having the opportunity to participate in an IB program is not inappropriate; however, if racially minoritized students—or any students—have been less prepared to be successful in those spaces, and/or if assignments to those programs have more to do with parent advocacy or students' performance of racial logics in ways that are considered "correct," then there is a problem. One intermediate step might be to create cohorts of racially minoritized students at early ages, upper elementary or middle school, who are supported to take more challenging coursework together. The combination of early preparation and peer support can be a powerful intervention in the short term. This would not in itself be a long-term intervention because it does not address the needs of students who are not selected to be in such a cohort. Rather, the goal should be to replicate those support programs throughout the curriculum so that all students are well prepared to enroll in whatever coursework they choose.

An important caveat to this point about tracking and structural factors has to do with the opportunity to inadvertently reinforce white racial logics in the process. In Ice's school, becoming a doctor or a lawyer was the only reputable pathway to success. Thus, the point is not to suggest to all students that they *should* enroll in an IB program or to set a goal to have all students enroll in honors classes. At least, not without being clear with students about the purpose of pursuing those opportunities. There is merit in providing high-quality instruction for all students to support them in whatever career path they might pursue. Students need a strong academic foundation in critical thinking skills, whether they plan to go to college, pursue career training, or take some other path.

When I say we should provide all students with a strong educational foundation, I mean that in addition to learning traditional academic disciplines, all students must be exposed to a more holistic set of academic offerings. Too few students receive robust lessons about their history. I did not learn any significant Black history until graduate school. A strong civics education is key. Further, some of the most useful skills I learned in high school came through our vocational technology program. However, taking those courses created challenges for my enrollment in advanced classes. It was always difficult to take courses across different "tracks," even though the courses were technically open to all students. This is an example of the ways in which tracking can occur as an unintended consequence of master scheduling.

Relationship factors highlight the importance of relationships with various stakeholders in the building, including teachers, but also school leaders and other staff (custodial staff, food service workers, bus drivers, counselors, etc.). Without a doubt, teachers played critical roles in students' experiences—for better and for worse. Rick shared that he was considered the teacher's pet, but personnel also made him feel obligated to drop his schoolwork whenever a guest visited the building and needed a tour. Emma felt that teachers were her closest friends, yet it was a teacher who laughed at her when she expressed a goal of attending an elite university. Understanding the deep impact that teachers and other school personnel have on students is certainly a feature of most educator preparation programs. However, most educators are unaware of the role we play in reproducing racial logics. With that awareness comes an understanding of the responsibility we have to work against these institutional processes. Part of that is an individual responsibility; however, it is also a responsibility to look at the collective impact of the adults in a school. For example, thinking about our school environment from a responsibility perspective brings a different reality to the lack of teachers from racially minoritized backgrounds: Does this send the message to white students and racially minoritized students that the only Black or Latinx adults in the school might be in service or support positions? Or does it send the message that the only teachers who talk about race are racially minoritized teachers? It is powerful to see examples of allyship from all teachers, a reflection of a collective commitment to anti-racist education at the individual teacher level, but also collectively as a reflection of the overall school climate. The key to that is in the people. These important people include those in the school, but also students' families and those in the broader community. It is important to bring in and meaningfully draw from the deep expertise found outside the school walls.[7]

UNDERSTANDING THE ROLE OF INTERSECTIONALITY AND CAPACITY FACTORS

I want to reiterate one important point about the role of capacity and intersectional factors. In the ROC framework, these aspects are integral to fully understanding the students' experiences and the ROC they incurred. Indeed, the earlier discussion of the three focal students highlighted just how imperative capacity and intersectional factors were in understanding the racial opportunity cost Micayla, Rick, and Emma experienced and the ways in which they were able to persevere through the challenges they faced. However, the primary relationship in the ROC framework is between school factors and racial opportunity cost, and this is for a reason. Intersectional and capacity factors are instrumental in our understanding, but when it comes to action, our focus must remain squarely focused on school factors. Those who are reading this book with the intention of using the ROC framework as a theoretical or analytical tool for research will need to be mindful of this larger framing and include the fuller understanding these mediating variables offer. However, as we think about the actions we need to take as educators to reduce racial opportunity cost, our greatest opportunity for meaningful change lies in those aspects of the school environment over which we have the most control: school factors.

I also want to be careful about the ways in which we bring in intersectional and capacity factors. These examinations must be within a larger systemic perspective lest we inadvertently move into deficit thinking and exacerbate the racial opportunity cost students experience by focusing on their resilience or bringing in third-party mentoring organizations to fix problems. In terms of the influence of capacity factors, yes, student resilience was an important factor and helping students foster those skills could be powerful in helping them achieve long-term academic success. However, those efforts must be carefully and explicitly accompanied by conversations with students that help them understand why these skills are necessary in the larger school and societal context. It is easy for even well-meaning efforts to nonetheless make students feel as though the issue is with them—that they should just be more resilient in order to be more successful, which would only potentially exacerbate their racial opportunity cost. The same is true of using third-party or nonprofit organizations. There was no doubt that these programs provided instrumental support to the students in our program. Indeed, without support from her leadership organization, Emma was sure that her path would not have led her to Northern College. However, relying *solely* on these organizations is also problematic. It again locates responsibility outside of the school and school personnel in a way that seems to absolve them of obligation. Therefore, efforts to foster these kinds of partnerships must be incorporated seamlessly into the school culture with full buy-in from school staff. Further, efforts must be made not to leave students behind because of lack of capacity or other procedural issues.

A similar point can be made about intersectional factors. Attention to the salience of race is critical, but not to the exclusion of students' other identities. We may see a student as Black, but then miss the many other aspects of their identity that are also critical to their experiences. Emma and Rick provided important examples of this point, as they both felt pride for their Puerto Rican heritage. However, Rick felt that those around him minimized or questioned his Puerto Rican identity because they only saw him as Black. Emma fought to be recognized as Puerto Rican rather than subsumed into a category of person of color or Latinx. Gender was also another layered identity that was salient in the students' experiences; even they noted the various ways in which race and gender contributed to meaningful differences in their experiences. Further, even as various social identities emerged from our analysis of the conversations we had with the students, we also recognized that there was much that did not surface. If we had more time with the students or had been able to build more rapport, I know they would have shared even more about the salience of sexual orientation, gender identity/gender expression, and other social identities that would have provided an even greater window into their experiences. I hope that future research will make this contribution to the ROC framework. Connecting to my earlier point, having a robust understanding of our students and their broader context is important for so much of our work as educators, but particularly so in our work to foster racial equity.

BROADER APPLICATIONS OF THE ROC FRAMEWORK

As I turn to closing thoughts, I want to expand the perspective more broadly to the larger implications of the racial opportunity cost framework. Until this point, most of the ROC work I have done has related specifically to the K–12 environment. However, as highlighted in the vignette that started this chapter, what we learned from the students in the project likely applies to other environments; after all, these white racial logics the students navigated exist for other populations, as well. For example, principals and superintendents from racially minoritized backgrounds are navigating the same racialized norms in predominantly white school settings as students. Can the ROC framework work with this population? What about for other groups, such as faculty from racially minoritized backgrounds? Do they experience racial opportunity cost? In what ways can the model change and adapt for use in other contexts, and what would we need to be mindful of in applying the ROC framework in these contexts?

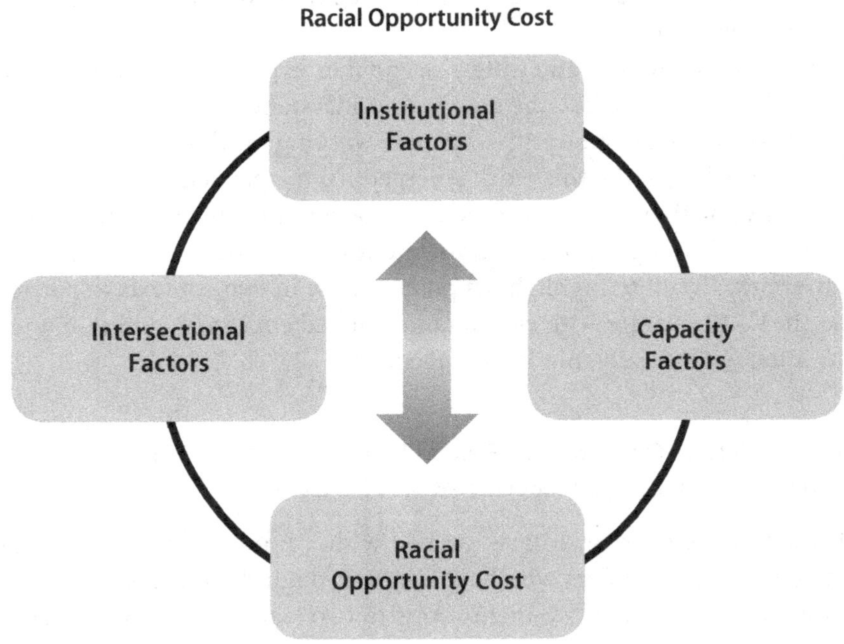

FIGURE 2 ROC Framework for Broader Use

Figure 2 looks very similar to the original ROC framework presented in the introductory chapter. However, what was "School Factors" is now labeled "Institutional Factors" (top of the graphic) to reflect its more general application. Institutions might include a university, workplace, or church or other religious setting. I have purposefully left broad the interpretation of "institution." Another difference between this graphic and the original ROC framework is the lack of themes or categories in each box. In the original ROC framework, the themes or categories of school factors and ROC came out of thematic analysis of our interviews with the students in our project. Even then, I have been clear that I never saw these categories as exhaustive of all the school factors, capacity factors, intersectionality factors, or racial opportunity costs that existed—there was room for additions based on the nuances that emerged from various contexts. In the case of this expanded framework, then, it is possible that some of the themes from the K–12 Black and Latinx student context may translate to other settings. Others may not. I imagine that a mix of some of the themes that emerged from the original ROC project would work well to characterize the experiences of racially minoritized individuals in other spaces, and some would not.

Overall, the ROC framework—original or expanded—is appropriate for use in contexts where the goal is to understand or describe the cost of success for racially minoritized people working in white-normed institutions. Further, while this work emerged from a particular U.S.-centric perspective, with tweaking, it could easily be modified to be used in global contexts. While I get excited about the myriad of possibilities for this framework, I want to highlight its potential use in two contexts in particular: in K–12 settings with racially minoritized educators, and in higher education with racially minoritized faculty.

APPLICATION ONE: K–12 PRACTITIONERS: TEACHERS, SCHOOL LEADERS, AND OTHER K–12 STAFF

Throughout my career, I have worked with a number of aspiring and practicing school leaders who have come through the leadership preparation programs at the two institutions in two states in which I worked. In that time, I have had numerous conversations with Black graduate students who are also working full-time as teachers and school leaders whose experiences could easily have been featured in the research in the article that opened this chapter. They have shared stories of having their knowledge and expertise questioned by white parents and teachers, told they were not a "good fit" for leadership, and faced an array of challenges as they navigated the white racial logics that were present in their schools and districts. When I taught about my work on racial opportunity cost, there was almost always a parallel conversation about the ways in which many of the themes from the research resonated with Black students in the class. Thus, it has always seemed appropriate to use the racial opportunity cost framework as a way of contextualizing the experiences of teachers and school leaders from racially minoritized backgrounds.

As I think about the ROC framework with this population in mind, I think some of the existing institutional factors themes may be useful. For example, climate factors almost certainly apply in a number of ways as teachers navigate racialized expectations of how they should dress, speak, and behave. I have often heard from Black teachers who felt that their school wanted the appearance of diversity, but in all other ways they were expected to fit the (white-normed) mold. Structural factors, too, likely have some relevance for an application of the ROC framework with Black educators. Dr. Darrius Stanley's research on "teacher tracking" or the ways in which Black teachers are summarily funneled into teaching lower-track classes and into disciplinary roles seems particularly applicable.[8] And I can imagine that relationships with fellow teachers and administrators would play the same complicated role of both exacerbating and alleviating the racial opportunity cost educators experience that emerged from the research with Black and Latinx students.

Speaking of racial opportunity cost, what similarities might there be between the existing framework and its application to K–12 practitioners from racially minoritized backgrounds? Again, I have to believe that there are some parallels. For example, teachers' feeling that their expertise was questioned by white peers and parents certainly aligned with representation costs. However, even as there were likely to be parallels, I also know that there will be points of departure. One issue that has emerged anecdotally from conversations with my students that would not be captured in the existing framework was the positioning of Black teachers between the system and their students. While these educators often felt beaten down by having to navigate the white logics that brought such tension, they also knew that however difficult it was for them, it was even more difficult for their Black students. Educators I have talked to expressed feelings of guilt over the idea of leaving their students, especially when there were very few other teachers from racially minoritized backgrounds in their school contexts. They also felt a deep sense of hypocrisy as reproducers of the white logics that they perpetuated as teachers, even as they also fought to dismantle those systems. Understanding more fully the ways in which Black educators make sense of that dual role could be a compelling contribution with this population using the ROC framework.

APPLICATION TWO: HIGHER EDUCATION

As I have worked on this project over the last ten years, I have had numerous conversations with colleagues about how the ROC framework elucidates their experiences in higher education. Indeed, several years ago, some colleagues and I shared the possibilities for the ROC framework for higher education at an American Educational Research Association conference. It has been impossible to do this work with K–12 students and not see parallels in my own experiences navigating the racialized expectations present in higher education, especially related to the tenure and promotion process. I have had personal encounters almost daily with the implications of white racial logics that deeply influenced my path as a Black, female professor, particularly early in my career before I earned tenure.

Although I have not conducted my own empirical study of the experiences of racially minoritized faculty using the ROC framework, as with the potential use of the ROC framework with K-12 educators from racially minoritized backgrounds shared earlier, I am equally confident that there are ways in which the institutional factors remain relevant in the higher education context. For example, in terms of climate, there is plenty of research that notes the ways in which notions of "fit" influence expectations for success.[9] Similarly, structural factors are likely relevant, but in a slightly different application if we look at understanding how racially minoritized faculty are impacted by racialized stratification, from the ways in which we are funneled into non-tenure track positions or out of positions where we are able to make policy and other structural change.[10] Similarly, I can see how relationship factors would be useful as faculty of color navigate peer relationships that are instrumental to success in achieving tenure, but where the same people can also sabotage the process.

Just as there are likely some parallels with institutional factors, there are likely also parallels with the racial opportunity cost that Black and Latinx faculty experience. In terms of psychosocial factors, there is a whole discipline around imposter syndrome in higher education.[11] The potential for representation costs also deeply resonates with me. As a Black, cisgendered woman, full professor at a Research 1 institution, I represent less than 1 percent of higher education faculty.[12] I am cognizant every day of my positionality in "representing" for Black faculty, but Black women full professors, in particular. This psychic responsibility is accompanied by a literal responsibility, as I am called upon to write an increasing number of tenure and promotion letters, given how few of us there are at this level.

There are also important new contributions to the ROC framework that would come from its use with higher education faculty. For example, on its face, it might seem that community costs apply in the same way as they do in the K–12 context. After all, the same racial logics that created separation for students from their families likely only become exacerbated as we navigate graduate school. On this note, I had a family member (lovingly) warn me when I was in graduate school that I would likely never get married. However, I do not think the existing "community costs" category fully captures the potential nuance of this issue for faculty from racially minoritized backgrounds, particularly for Black women. Black women remain the most educated population in this country, but that success comes at a cost that extends beyond a potential separation or strain with the larger Black community. What are the nuances of that cost? What does it mean for Black women who achieve so much but at such a high price? That issue is an element of the ROC framework that is not currently reflected but one for which I see potential in future research.

FINAL ROC CLOSING THOUGHTS

Throughout this book, I have worked to make a case for understanding the role of school factors in the challenges faced by Black and Latinx students in white-normed schools—to elucidate the costs they incurred as a result of pursuing academic success in schools imbedded with white racial logics. A central feature of my argument in this chapter and the heart of the ROC framework is the interplay between school factors and their impact on Black and Latinx students. These school factors are purposefully difficult to see but are nonetheless instrumental in a full understanding of what these students experienced. Along the way, I have urged readers not to focus on individual actions, but to rather see them for the representation of the larger system. I have reinforced the message that addressing the actions of individual racist actors locates the problem in the wrong place, further deflecting attention from the systemic issues present. I stand by the importance of this shifted perspective. However, I want now to turn away from this macro systemic perspective to that of the most micro: the individual person. As certain as I am, based on the research that forms the foundation for this book, that what happens in schools is a reflection of historically longstanding institutionalized practices, I am just as certain that if we have a chance at making meaningful change it will start—must start—with what we do as individuals.

When I say it "starts" with individuals, I really mean with internal work. This is a lesson I have learned from teaching about these issues in my leadership preparation courses. One of the most meaningful changes I have made in my leadership for social justice class is to start with an assignment that challenges students to talk about themselves through the lens of their racial identity, a racial autobiography. The assignment offers a critical opportunity for all of my students. It is important for my students from racially minoritized backgrounds because, despite feeling more comfortable talking about race and looking at the world through a racial lens, they have often not learned that there are words—indeed, whole fields of study—that offer perspective and meaning to their experiences. The assignment is obviously also important for my white students for whom race is not something they have often ever identified with personally. "I don't have a culture," they often said. Before incorporating this assignment into the course, I started the class by providing a historical perspective on the development and foundation of institutionalized racism. I also taught a crash course in the history of Black education and other racially minoritized groups, as too few students had been exposed to this history. The frustration I had that led me to eventually adopt this racial autobiography assignment was that at the end of the semester, many white students had a fuller understanding of racial issues, their historical origins, and their connections to contemporary educational issues. However, they also still often retained the belief that race was something that racially minoritized people had. They did not fully connect with race on a personal level. They were more open to the topic of anti-racism and committed to action after taking the course, but too often this was from the perspective of wanting to help their Black and Latinx students and other racially minoritized people. Of course, this is a world-view that is difficult to shift after just one course. Indeed, racial identity was not something many of my white students had ever thought about because it was not a lens through which they viewed the world. They did not need to, because the white racial logics that permeate our society make certain this will be the case. Indeed, *guarantee* it to be so. Thus, I started using this assignment and the purposeful conversations that accompanied it to ground the course in a sense of personal identity and responsibility.

When students share their assignments and what they learned by doing it, I am not surprised to hear my racially minoritized students talk easily and openly about their experiences. These are issues they are used to thinking and talking about every day. Maybe not in formal settings, but certainly at home and with friends. This is often shocking to white students, who have not had the need nor opportunity to do so. When they try to talk about their racial identity, the stories they share often feature them in supporting roles to racially minoritized people who are the real focus of the story. "I gave a ride to a homeless Latinx person once and then I saw him get arrested," they might start. Or, "I will never forget when a peer called our Black classmate the N-word and I did not know how to respond," is another typical response. When I push them to redirect to a personal story where their racial identity is featured, they find themselves unable to do so, and the resulting conversations are awkward, stilted, and full of discomfort and concern about misusing terms. "What does that mean, then?" I'll ask them. "What does it mean that your Black classmates are able to share these kinds of stories but you cannot? What does this say about the way you have experienced the world?" I do not ask this in a critical way, but out of genuine curiosity about what their response will be. Responding to that question often unlocks the deeper understanding that helps them engage with these topics in a more personal way. By the end of the semester, though, students are decidedly more comfortable talking about race. What's the magic potion here? Am I just a master at helping students open up? Definitely not. It is shocking how little experience we have in talking openly about race. Even a little experience can make an appreciable difference.

Recall that the students in my leadership for social justice class are teachers, principals, and central office administrators in their regular life. I think they are fairly representative of most educators in their discomfort with addressing racial issues, and that is on us, as teacher and leadership preparation programs sending our students into schools without this foundation. Recall the story I shared in the preface of this book about a superintendent from a local district who had made racist comments about George Floyd. He received his doctorate from our program, and that was something we needed to face and take responsibility for as a faculty. However, because educators are not trained to talk about race, they are not trained to foster environments where students feel comfortable talking about race. Further, students cannot gain those skills, either, without the proper support from school personnel. It was overwhelmingly evident in our conversations with the students in the ROC project that they did not have access to spaces where they could talk about race and racism. They may have had a teacher here or there who provided a welcomed opportunity in their class, or a particular extracurricular club that provided the space, but rarely were these opportunities cultivated as a sustained and expected practice in their schools.

This brings me back to my point about individual awareness and action—the responsibility we all have regardless of the specific position we hold: teachers, counselors, principals, superintendents, etc. Working to create schools that are supportive of Black and Latinx students and all students with minoritized identities will require us to work purposefully against the white logics that permeate our environments. Indeed, students engage with the institutional factors and white logics *through* us as educators, as individuals. We unknowingly transmit these logics unless we are intentional in our efforts to be more aware. The purpose of pointing out the institutional framework is not to absolve ourselves of responsibility. We do not say, "Oh well, racism is here and there is nothing I can do about it." Rather, this knowledge should *emphasize* our role and our responsibility. We must be cognizant of the position we play as agents in this system so that we can be prepared to respond differently and proactively dismantle the system. As we reflect on all the stories the students shared, what stands out are the people: the people who perpetuated harm, like the teacher who laughed at Emma when she expressed her aspiration to attend Harvard. Or the teachers and school leaders who did nothing to substantively respond to the series of racist incidents at Rick's school. Or the teacher who did not notice how difficult it was for Micayla to just be herself when white students were taunting her for saying "It ain't broke."

The ROC framework is a tool. Its value relies on people using it effectively. That is the key. I provide the nuance in the framework and elucidate the issues of school factors, capacity factors, intersectionality factors, and racial opportunity costs not because there is magic in these four categories. Indeed, I have invited readers to take wide latitude in modifying the framework as they feel fits, to *empower* educators to use the ROC framework as a tool to proactively cultivate change. The other reality is that even if we were able to perfectly implement the ROC framework, which is not possible, doing so would not inoculate a school or district from perpetuating racism or ensure that Black and Latinx students would not experience racial opportunity cost. However, that is not the point. The point of the ROC framework is to provide nuanced information to help those who are in positions to make change in schools to better understand how, regardless of our intention, we may unwittingly be making it more difficult for students from racially minoritized backgrounds to do well in school, to be cognizant of the ways in which we increase their racial opportunity cost, even if we do not mean to do so.

There is hope here. I know none of us could do this work if we did not possess a fundamental optimism. I could not work with future school leaders or serve on my local school board if I did not have a deep conviction in our ability to foster meaningful change. If I have learned anything in the twenty or so years that I have worked in education, it is this: if there is any hope to cultivate a more equitable society, educators are the people to do it and schools are the place where we can get it done. Let's get to work.

ROC Talk: Reflections from the Original ROC Research Team Members

Drs. Leslie Locke, Rhonda Fowler, and Kristin Huggins

A note from Terah Venzant Chambers: I was thrilled when Drs. Locke, Fowler, and Huggins agreed to share their reflections in a ROC Talk for this book. I extended to them the opportunity to write a reflection along with a request to review an early draft of the book. It was important to add their perspective. They had been there for the data collection; they knew these students and had been there every step of the way. Unsurprisingly, they offered critical insights and nuance that I had forgotten in the passage of time. Reading their reflections here takes me back to highlights of the research project—stimulating conversations over long car rides and steaming cups of coffee. Of course, while I am flattered by their positive reflections on my role as a mentor, it was not something I had expected them to cover (they knew, but insisted on including it anyway).

LESLIE ANN LOCKE

Locke's Reflections on Being Part of the ROC Research Team

Being a member of the original team that collected the data related to Terah Venzant Chambers's first study of racial opportunity cost (ROC) was an important piece in my development as a scholar and a mentor. Like the other team members, I was a graduate student then, about midway through a PhD. By then, I had taken a couple of classes with Venzant Chambers, and she had signed on as a member of my dissertation committee.

At that time, few faculty in the department were known to invite students to work with them on their research teams. Terah, at that time, was not too far from the graduate student experience herself and understood the importance of graduate students obtaining some hands-on research experience before collecting their own data for their dissertations and entering the job market. I jumped at the chance to work with Terah, Rhonda, and Kristin on the ROC team.

Based on her own experiences in school and her previous research, Terah had already troubled the concept of "racial opportunity cost." By the time she had conceived of the original research study, she had identified some colleges to contact; however, as a team, we were all involved in much of the remaining decision making, including the design of the interview protocols, recruiting, data collection, transcription, analysis, and publication. On the whole, participating on the research team was an invaluable experience for me as a graduate student. Further, and as with most qualitative studies, the most interesting aspect was data collection. The students who graciously shared their time and perspectives with us at Northern College and Southern College, were in a word, amazing. I remain honored that they chose to hang out with us for a couple of days, share their stories, and think critically with us about their high school experiences and the policies and practices of schools.

Based on my own experiences in high school and those of my immediate family, I understand high school can be a problematic place. Those who are supposed to support students, often don't. Doors to advancement are typically narrow, not broad. Quality teachers who care about students are more rare than they are common. Students who do not make it out of high school with a degree are likely to face a slew of related challenges throughout their lives. I have seen and experienced such challenges firsthand.

The ROC students, however, were high achievers. Their good grades opened and broadened some doors to supportive teachers, advanced placement, and quality instruction. However, they also reported that their experiences were negated by their educators' personal racism and their schools' institutional racism. These experiences with racism in their schools "cost" the students in a variety of different ways. The one-way assimilation forces of schools are uniquely experienced by students of Color. The ROC participants examined these forces with us, shedding light on how those forces impacted them and discussing how they negotiated and challenged various ways in which to move forward toward their goals. Other scholars have noted that students are the best informants of their own experiences.[1]

While such a declaration seems like it should be obvious, much scholarship continues to make claims about policies and practices in schools yet never analyzes students' experiences or perceptions. I remain honored to have been privy to the ROC participants' stories and to have learned of their experiences directly. Further, I understand my good fortune to have interacted with the data and to have coauthored scholarship related to racial opportunity costs alongside Terah, Rhonda, and Kristin.

I learned a lot from my experience on Terah's research team. Certainly, I gained practical research skills and experience; however, perhaps more importantly, I saw a faculty member treat the student researchers on her team as equals, as intelligent women with their own educational background, scholarly interests, and research experience. Terah mentored us as budding scholars, allowing us to work through the project and the data with her, rather than for her. I hope the students who now work with me can say the same.

Locke's Personal Interactions with Systemic Whiteness (Critical White Supremacy)

As a white person, I remain able to maneuver the world differently than folks of Color. In our racist society, I benefit daily in uncountable ways from my race. My social class background and gender, while certainly marginalized in our society, are secondary or tertiary or quaternary . . . appearing far down this list, when compared to race.

As a first generation high school graduate, I developed an eye for inequities early—particularly those related to socioeconomic status.[2] I saw the school system underserve and dismiss my family. We bear scars from those school experiences, generations deep. It was not until graduate school, however, that I began to more critically think about race and racism. What would be my family's scars if we had to also consider how our race and our educators' racism would impact us? We did not have to carry this concern. We did not have to think about schooling in the same ways as the ROC students did—what will an advanced class *cost* me in terms of who I am? What will partaking in the school extracurriculars *cost* me in terms of who I am? What will following the (perhaps misguided) advice of school advisors and counselors *cost* me in terms of who I am, and what will be the potential future missed opportunities? Our education systems continue to largely benefit white students from middle- and high-income families. These students do not have to consider how or what their experience in public K–12 schools will *cost* them in terms of who they are.

Asking critical questions such as these and directed at our public education systems is at the heart of my research agenda. I am after learning from those who interact with education systems and from those who are impacted by them, and ultimately working collaboratively to improve education systems such that one day they do not impose costs for any students.

Locke's Personal Applications of ROC

Beyond publishing the original articles with Terah, I was also able to apply some of the original ROC study data alongside data that I had collected from my dissertation study.[3] Here, we used data collected with participants from both studies who identified as Latina. While the ROC students were high achievers, the students who participated in my dissertation study were underperforming, according to the school administrators. As a research team, we took these two data sets and reviewed them for aspects of racial opportunity cost, alongside Yosso's framework of community cultural wealth.[4] Yosso's framework consists of six forms of capital (aspirational, resistant, social, navigational, familial, and linguistic) that students of Color carry with them into educational spaces. We used both frameworks to identify the "costs and capitals" of schooling for Latina students. That is, we asked, what are the capitals or strengths that Latina students bring with them to the school space, and what are the barriers or costs they face once there? Our findings indicate that the norms of school and the norms students embrace play a critical role in creating conditions for a positive school experience.

I continue to suggest the opus of the ROC work to graduate students who are interested in better understanding students' experiences in K–12 spaces, particularly those of students from systemically marginalized groups.

Being on the original research team was a valuable and rewarding experience in so many ways. However, I would be remiss not to reiterate the fact that Terah not only allowed us to share in a very important research experience, she also taught us how to be good mentors. Good mentors are often hard to find in higher education, and Terah was an excellent one. She provided not only opportunities, but guidance. She was there for the celebrations, surely, but she was also there when the chips were down. She listened and helped to devise a path forward. I have learned, and continue to learn, from Terah. Thank you, Terah, for showing us how it's done.

RHONDA FOWLER

Fowler's Reflections on Being Part of the ROC Research Team

I was a new African American doctoral student who had no experience with research when Dr. Venzant Chambers took me under her wing and provided me with an opportunity of a lifetime. The opportunity to work not only with Terah, but also with Kristin and Leslie, was instrumental in my development as a researcher. My position as a graduate researcher not only helped inform my dissertation, but also the work I continue to do as it relates to social justice, equity, and inclusion. I recall when I was searching for a graduate assistantship as a graduate fellow reviewing many of the faculty in my department. Dr. Venzant Chambers kept standing out. Her current research was interesting, and the fact that she decided to take me on as student was exciting.

As I stated before, I was brand new to research and "wet behind the ears." I didn't understand the significance of interviewing, transcribing, and analyzing the data, but Dr. Venzant Chambers gave me the opportunity to get my hands wet the moment I stepped foot in the program. As we began to prepare for the project—working on the IRB, awaiting approval, sending out emails to participants, scheduling the interviews, conducting the interviews (individual and focus), and analyzing the data—I recall telling myself, "This isn't too bad," not realizing this was all part of qualitative research.

Again, at the time, I was brand new to the program and had no idea of what qualitative research was. However, I recall taking my first research course, and I remember saying to myself, "Oh, I've already done that" or "I know what that means." Dr. Venzant Chambers had exposed to me to qualitative research many semesters before I had the opportunity to take my first course. Many of my peers had not received this type of hands-on experience, and I was extremely grateful that she gave me the chance to be a part of the team.

As we continued with the project, I began to realize my passion: qualitative research was my niche. I enjoyed meeting new people, listening to their stories, and learning how their experiences impacted who they were. This was very intriguing to me, and I couldn't wait to start my own research project or to narrow down my dissertation topic. I am forever grateful for the experience. These high-achieving students came from all walks of life and wanted to succeed in their undergraduate program. It was interesting to hear about where they came from, how they got to where they are, and what their plans were moving forward.

Having real-life, hands-on experience not only aided and supported me during my program, but it has also informed how I conduct research. Now that I am a faculty member, I apply what I learned from the team (Drs. Venzant Chambers, Locke, and Huggins) to my work. I remind my students that it is ok to step outside of their comfort zone and take on challenges. These challenges only make you stronger. The challenge that Dr. Venzant Chambers afforded me has made me a much stronger researcher, faculty member, and mentor to my students.

Fowler's Personal Anecdotes about Early Realizations of Whiteness, White Supremacy, and the Systemic-Institutionalized Perpetuation of Barriers to Success

I come from a family where few attended college. I am first-generation student in many ways: the first in my family to obtain a degree, and the first to obtain a graduate degree, including a master's and doctorate. During my time in K–12 schools, my school district was about 30 percent African American, 15 percent Hispanic, and 55 percent white. I recall as a middle school student that I took a standardized test that was required by the state of Texas. I was not a great test taker but did well in my classes. On this particular test, I didn't score well. I recall that my eighth-grade counselor, a middle-aged white woman, asked my parents and me to meet with her. She told us that based on my scores, the furthest that I could move forward in post-graduation (college) would be a two-year technical college or some type of technical certificate. I walked away defeated and believing her. I also recall my parents telling me that this was not my reality. Regardless of what the counselor had told me, I was much better than that. I always kept this in the back of my head as I progressed through school: in my mind, my counselor knew what she was taking about, but my parents, on the other hand, were my advocates and my support, telling me I was much better than what she had stated.

This idea of systemic whiteness was at work. Many of the Black students or students of color were always seen as unable to succeed academically but able to perform well athletically. I recall only a few African American students in our class who were voted as those who would succeed after graduation; the others were all white. There must be allies against those who support these issues of racism and the idea of not supporting all students. It's critical to the success of students. In my case, if I didn't have supportive parents, I would have allowed what my white counselor told me to determine my destiny.

At the time, I didn't see this as systemic whiteness. I only saw it as my counselor giving me sound advice, when in actuality, she wasn't. She wasn't supporting my journey. She didn't offer my parents and me resources that could possibly assist me in test taking and help me over those most crucial next few years of school—those years that really start to define what your college future may look like. However, I am happy to say that I defeated the odds. A close friend and classmate, an African American male, and I both earned our degrees (undergraduate and graduate) from predominantly white institutions (PWIs) and teach at PWIs. I am also happy to say that many other students of color not just from our high school class but from other classes graduated and now have successful careers. We must credit those who supported our journey. Our allies—our parents, school board members, and community members—who ensured that we all had access to an equitable education, including the rigorous and advanced classes.

How Fowler Applies the ROC Framework in Her Teaching and Research

This idea of systemic racism and systemic whiteness is real, and we must continue to advocate for our students of color. Currently, I am working with a friend and colleague (who I mentioned previously) who currently serves as the assistant superintendent in our former school district. He has implemented a program of academic success geared toward students of color. This program invites high school graduates of color who are now successful in their careers to come back and speak to current students of color about their experiences and how they got to where they are. It's an opportunity to encourage these students that they too can be successful without diminishing or downplaying who they. There are individuals out there who want to see them succeed and want to support their journey.

Currently as a clinical assistant professor at a PWI, I have the opportunity to teach undergraduate students and also serve as their mentor. Many students have approached me and indicated that they are not sure they can stay at our university. They have expressed their concern about not seeing many others in the classrooms and around campus who look like them, including faculty. Some have expressed their concerns of trying to fit in and be something they aren't. My role as a faculty member is to continue to advocate for these students, to be their ally and continue to work to dismantle systematic racism. Additionally, I serve on several diversity, equity, and inclusion committees within the department and college—continuing this work of dismantling systematic racism (whiteness). I must say this work is hard, but it's needed, and I am happy that we have many who have committed to this work.

KRISTIN HUGGINS

Huggins's Reflections on Being a Part of the ROC Research Team

I remember the first time Terah and I had the opportunity to discuss racial opportunity cost (ROC). It was the fall of 2007, and we were driving from College Station to Houston, where I was co-teaching the Foundations of Educational Administration course in the Houston Ed.D. cohort with Terah, who was the main instructor. We had a roundtrip of about three hours to discuss the concept and how we had seen it manifest in our personal and professional experience. For Terah, it was her personal experience as a high-achieving Black K–12 student. For me, it was reflecting back on my personal experience as a high-achieving white K–12 student and my professional experience of being a K–12 pre-Advanced Placement (AP) and AP English/Language Arts teacher. My personal experiences as a high-achieving K–12 white student in the late 1980s included fewer Black and Latinx students in my classes than when I was a K–12 Pre-AP and AP teacher in the late 1990s and early 2000s.

When Terah received some funding and started the ROC project in the late 2000s, I was curious to learn what a large group of high-achieving Black and Latinx students with various K–12 experiences would say was the racial opportunity cost they paid for being high achieving. Specifically, I was wondering if they thought the racial opportunity cost they paid was worth a cost-benefit analysis. At the time, as a fourth-year doctoral student, my thinking was somewhat scientifically instrumental. That is, I had yet to interact with Rick and Ice and Rita and Emma—whose faces I can see even today among the other students who shared their ROC experiences with us.

Being a part of the ROC research team meant unpacking my own racial identity and positionality. We spent some time discussing identities and positionalities in the ROC project as a team, which meant that we were all willing to make the students in the project as comfortable as possible with strangers. At the design phase, this included incorporating both individual and focus group interviews. I had never been a part of a research study that included focus group interviews, and the ROC project illuminated for me the added nuance provided by incorporating this form of data collection, especially after each participant had the opportunity to convey their individual experiences. Through the focus group interviews, I was able to see how at ease this form of data collection made some of the students feel when explicating their experiences further than they had in their individual interviews. Additionally, the ROC research team discussed how we would interview the students individually. The four of us were sitting at a table in one of the rooms that had been provided for us by the two universities. We paid attention to whom the students engaged with first and tried to match that individual with that student for the individual interview. We also tried to interview in teams, if at all possible, in order to sense-make the interviews together prior to the focus group interviews. Again, we were very intentional about acknowledging our identities and positionalities and wanted, above all, for the students to feel comfortable conveying their experiences.

Huggins's Personal Anecdotes about Her Early Realizations of Whiteness, White Supremacy, and the Systemic-Institutionalized Perpetuation of Barriers to Success

Part of acknowledging our identities included recalling how we had come to understand the racial opportunity costs in our personal and professional experience. While during my doctoral coursework, I had had multiple courses on social justice, race, and identity, most of my graduate school learning was theoretical, not experiential. However, prior to attending graduate school to attain my doctorate, I had been a secondary English/language arts (ELA) teacher for eleven years in various K–12 schools.

At one of those schools, my high school alma mater, when I was hired, the ELA Department Chair explained to me that all teachers in the department had the opportunity to teach an honors or Advanced Placement course, but that all teachers in the department also had to teach Writing 101. Writing 101 was a remedial course that students had to take if they had failed to pass the school district's writing assessment in their junior year of high school. I explained to the ELA Department Chair that I felt confident I could teach students wherever they were in developing their knowledge and skills as writers and readers. In my first year as a teacher at the school, I taught a section of pre-AP sophomore English. In that class, I had sixteen students: two of them were students of color, one Black male and one Black/Asian male. The following year, I taught a section of Writing 101. I remember the first day of that class. It was first period, and I stood at the door to greet my new students. As each student came into the classroom, I checked their names on the class roster. After the bell rang to start class, I walked into the room. I paused. I had seen the students come through the door. I had checked their names on the class roster. But at that moment, as I looked across the classroom, I noticed that all thirteen students were Black. At the time, the high school was approximately 33 percent students of color. After teaching at the school for two years, I knew writing struggles were not particular to a certain student racial demographic. So, why was there only one student racial demographic in Writing 101?

My experience teaching Writing 101 did not give me the language and understanding of systemic inequities that my doctoral classes provided in graduate school. However, every time a conception of social justice, race, and identity and the ways in which districts and schools systemically perpetuate inequities arose in one of my classes, I remembered Writing 101. I had lived that systemic inequity reality. I had lived it in my hometown at my high school alma mater. That experience had made me realize that my own education probably would have been very different as a Black female at my high school. My white privilege protected me from that alternative.

How Huggins Applies the ROC Framework in Her Teaching and Research

Being a doctoral student at Texas A&M University during the time of the ROC project provided me with a space within the Department of Educational Administration and Human Resource Development, where equity and social justice were centered. At the time, Dr. James Joseph Scheurich, who had written extensively about racial topics, including anti-racist education and coloring epistemologies, was the Department Chair. He would subsequently become my dissertation advisor.[5] One of the major learnings that occurred during our time together as dissertation advisor and advisee was the acknowledgment that I needed to find my own place in anti-racist, equity-focused work. While I was a part of the research articles that came from the ROC project, my research has not continued to focus on anti-racist work.[6] Instead, I have chosen to leverage my white privilege in spaces where it is afforded breadth, specifically in the hiring decisions within the academy of those who are much more eloquent and have the lived experience to be the role models for the individuals we need to see in educational leadership positions in schools. I spend much of my time now coordinating programs. One of these is a principal preparation program. The research is rather clear on the influence of people of color in education providing the model for future generations.[7] As Terah mentions, she wants to be the example of the educators she never saw for future generations of scholars.

Beyond my focus on the human resource aspects of equity, the programs for which I am responsible as program coordinator are continuously working toward increasing equity. For example, we changed our scheduling in one of our programs when students provided feedback that our current scenario created unnecessary burdens on certain demographic groups of students. Similar to many educational leadership programs across the United States, we have doctoral courses called Leadership for Social Justice and Race, Representation, and Identity. Leadership for Social Justice is one of the first courses students take in our doctoral program. Because the academic setting is in what is considered a progressive state, these concepts resonate with many of our students. However, social justice leadership as a practice, for many of our students, is more aspirational than actual. That is, educational leadership, especially at the upper levels in educational organizations, has been, and continues to be, vexed with power and politics. While our students have the best of intentions, the hard labor of enacting social justice is much more of a heavy lift than they anticipate. Thus, I, along with colleagues, work to assist our students in moving forward in the next step of doing social justice work in the contexts of their varied school districts.

Terah Venzant Chambers's Take

There is so much to take in from the reflections that Leslie, Rhonda, and Kristin offered here about the early conceptions of the ROC work, their involvement in the project, and the ways in which their work has continued and evolved in the years since the project ended. Their reflection on the early days of the project took me back to a time where the racial opportunity cost concept was new; I was full of hope but also uncertainty. Until I read her reflection, I had forgotten about those long car rides with Kristin as we traveled to teach in the Houston suburbs; I talked through my emergent ideas, and Kristin asked questions that helped me refine my thinking. Rhonda was the newest to the research process, as she mentioned, but was instrumental in keeping us organized. Leslie came to the team after Kristin and Rhonda, as I recall, but her deep work around critical whiteness was a crucial addition.

I am mindful, also, that their involvement in the work continued after the data collection was over. Analyzing and writing up the data for publication was a years-long endeavor. Working on collaborations that joined the ROC work with their research, like the project Leslie mentioned, was another highlight of the project. Overall, however, I am grateful for their dedication. Their questions, insights, and overall commitment to the work contributed to the strength of the project. Throughout the process, I have wanted most of all for this work to reflect the experiences of the many racially minoritized students whose stories did not seem to be reflected in existing research. However, with all "new" things, there is a danger in stepping into new territory. Was I characterizing the students' perspectives accurately? Was I honoring them in an authentic way? Kristin, Leslie, and Rhonda were there to help ask these questions with me. I, of course, fully own any mistakes that we made along the way, but certainly know that this work would not be what it is without their insights.

Collaborative research is messy; there were certainly times where as a group we made decisions about research design or analysis that differed a bit from what I would have chosen. We had spirited discussions about the themes and storylines that developed, especially in those early days. However, it was important to me as a mentor to fully involve them in the process and that meant—within reason—yielding to the group and coming to consensus. I came to appreciate those early days later in the process, when I was writing sole-authored manuscripts based on this work, and certainly as I revisited all of the data for analysis for this book project. I longed to talk things out with the team, to disagree but then find common ground, to celebrate the way a story came together from the students' voices. Although I wrote this book "alone," it is certainly a testament to the power of collaborative research, the value of mentoring, and the unmitigated joy that can be found in qualitative research.

APPENDIX A

Methodological Note

INTRODUCTION

As noted at various times throughout the text, I have published a number of peer-reviewed articles based on the empirical research that forms the foundation for this book. Rather than repeat that theoretical, epistemological, and methodological information, I will point those interested in those details to prior published work[1] and focus here on the general design of the study and what fueled some of the decisions we made.

ORIGINS OF THE RESEARCH DESIGN

When I first began to conceptualize the research design of this project, some fifteen years ago, I thought a lot about who the participants would be. Ideally, it would be students at different high schools who could speak to the ways in which they were impacted by their educational environments. However, in my previous research with high school students in tracked math and English classes, it took months of conversations before they began to see the institutional influences on their experiences. It was not their fault—they just were not used to looking at those issues. The students were thinking often for the first time about issues that had been purposely hidden and it took time for their thinking to evolve. I did not have that kind of time available for this project, nor did I have the capacity to travel to a number of different high schools to acquire the kind of variation in the sample that I desired.

I eventually came to a solution that would address both of these problems. I decided to involve first- and second-year college students. Their having been away from high school—but not for too long—might "jump start" their ability to take a more critical perspective of their experiences. Also, by targeting college students, I would not have to travel to multiple high schools. As I thought more about it, I realized this approach could solve a third problem with which I had been wrestling: how to define "high achieving" for the purposes of the project. If we chose colleges that were already defined as highly selective, we could side-step the question of how we might determine whether these students were academically successful. In addition, these kinds of colleges pride themselves on fostering geographic and other kinds of diversity, and so students from these colleges would have come from a variety of high schools. The variation in high school type would help us tell a story about the students' experiences that transcended their individual high school environments. That is, I did not want a narrative that could be dismissed as something that just happened in suburban schools or that occurred as a result of a few bad actors.

It was also important to me to involve graduate students in the research process. I reached out to some of the advanced graduate students in the department with whom I had developed close relationships. Rhonda Fowler, Kristin Huggins, and Leslie Locke became instrumental members of the team, contributing to the research design process in meaningful ways. The time we spent together as a research team is among some of my fondest memories of my tenure at Texas A&M University.

SITE SELECTION

Identifying two colleges to target for data collection was a fairly straightforward process; we knew we wanted to choose elite colleges that fared well in the *U.S. News & World Report* rankings to help with the definition of high-achieving students for the project. From there, we selected one university (Southern College) because it was within a reasonable driving distance of our university. This made it easier to return as a research team on additional trips. We had to travel by plane to the Midwest to visit the second university (Northern College), but I went forward with it because of the strong connections I had with people there who could help reserve space for our interviews and identify students who might be interested in participating in the project. Both universities had relatively diverse student populations, which meant that we hoped to recruit a good number of Black and Latinx students. With our sites selected, we moved on to thinking about who we wanted to be in the study and how they should be involved.

PARTICIPANT SELECTION AND RECRUITMENT

We advertised at both colleges through existing racial affinity groups for Black and Latinx students as well as through word-of-mouth recruiting.[2] We hoped to build a robust pool of students at each university, and were for the most part successful. We were interested in students who generally identified racially as Black/African American and/or Latinx and who also self-identified as "high-achieving"—whatever that meant to them. At Southern College, we talked with seven students: two Latinx students, Carmen (Hispanic) and Syril (Mexican), and five Black students, Gregg (African American), Jessica (African American), Melody (African American), Micayla (African American), and Rita (Black).[3] Eleven students participated from Northern College. One student, Rick, identified both as Black and Latinx (Biracial, Puerto Rican/Black). Four students identified as Latinx: Adriana (Latina), Araceli (Mexican American), Emma (Puerto Rican), and Lillie (Latina/Mexican). Six students identified as Black: Alexa (African American/Dominican), Carla (African American), Elsie (African American/Eritrean), Ice (African American), Moe (African American), and Zion (African American). In total, eighteen students participated in our project across the two sites.

DATA COLLECTION AND ANALYSIS

Southern College

Our primary data collection technique was individual and focus group interviews with all of the students. We headed to Southern College first and conducted batches of interviews over the course of several weeks. For the Black students, we set up a focus group once all of the individual interviews had been conducted at a time that was mutually agreeable for students and the research team. We had a little more trouble finding Latinx students to participate in the study. Our greatest success in recruiting came after attending a racial affinity group meeting for Latinx-identified students on campus. We were able to interview Carmen and Syril right after that meeting. However, our failure to recruit more Latinx students over the several weeks we traveled back and forth to Southern College eventually led us to decide not to schedule a focus group with just two students. Thus, we held a focus group interview only with Black students at Southern College.

Northern College

We had to be more strategic in our approach to data collection at Northern College because we hoped to conduct all of the interviews in one visit. With limited funds and four people to accommodate as part of the research team, we had to be thoughtful about cost. At the same time, we were committed to returning to Northern College as many times as necessary. Despite being farther away from Northern College, our internal contacts there were stronger than at Southern College, so we had help recruiting a number of students in advance of our trip, and a few more signed up to participate while we were on campus. As with our approach at Southern College, we conducted individual interviews with the students first and then scheduled focus groups for the Black and Latinx students separately, on the back end of the trip. Thus, we held two focus groups at Northern College. Because he identified as Black and Latinx, Rick had his choice of focus groups. He chose the Latinx focus group because he said it worked better for his schedule.

Although our primary data collection came through the individual and focus group interviews, we also relied fairly heavily on document collection and analysis. In particular, we spent a lot of time looking at the websites of the high schools the students attended, trying to get a sense of the size, demographics, and any other information that would help us better understand the environment from which they came. We learned the most about these high schools from the students themselves, but it was important for us to try and fill in the gaps with direct research, as well.

Again, while we used fairly traditional data analysis techniques, we spent considerable time talking together as a research team about what we wanted to do and why. I did this in part because the graduate students were learning more about qualitative research by *doing* it, and I wanted them to be involved in all aspects of the process. We approached the analysis process as a team, using techniques that they had learned in their qualitative methods courses. We probably "over-engineered" this part of the process, with every member of the team being involved in transcribing, re-transcribing, and coding all of the interview data. At each new stage in the process, we would meet as a group first, working together until we had calibrated our approach, and then divide the remaining work up among the team. However, even as we took this "divide and conquer" approach, I always reviewed all of the work myself as the leader of the team. This certainly took more time, but led to the team having a much more in-depth understanding of the data.

ETHICAL CONSIDERATIONS

I have always in my heart been drawn to qualitative research methods. The search for meaning and the focus on storytelling have always been compelling to me. Because mentoring graduate students was also essential to me, I worked hard to involve them in a significant way without placing an undue burden on them from a workload perspective. As we discussed various methodological options, I made sure we were leading with purpose and intention, designing a study that would best set us up to understand the students' experiences of navigating academic success in their white-normed schools.

In addition to navigating issues related to research design while working with a team of graduate students, I needed to attend to the racial and other demographic considerations of a team consisting of two Black people and two white people, all of whom identified as women. Although working with the graduate students provided an essential mentoring opportunity, I was ever-mindful of my role as the principal investigator and my responsibility to "own" all of the decisions made in the project. As a result, when at all possible, I led the interviews we did with students, though the second interviewer was fully empowered to participate by asking questions and following up on lines of conversation. I was also intentional about never involving more than two members of the research team (usually me and one other person) in the individual interviews. After all, we had not met any of the students before, and we wanted them to feel as comfortable as possible. Facing an interview team of four strangers seemed like it would be a bit much.

There were a few occasions when, due to scheduling constraints, we had to interview students at the same time. Another member of the research team would lead those interviews. In those cases, I made sure the other team of two was also mixed in terms of racial demographics: at least one Black and one white member of the team always conducted each interview. As a research team, we spent a lot of time talking about all of the aspects of the project; the role of our racial identities was a frequent topic. What did it mean for the white members of the research team to talk with Black and Latinx students about their experiences navigating the white-normed expectations they encountered in school? On a few occasions, students clearly hesitated to say something about a white teacher or school leader for fear of offending the white members of our team. For their part, Locke and Huggins were very proactive in addressing this issue directly and from the start, helping put students at ease to talk more freely about their experiences. Still, as with all qualitative research, I know these and other dynamics influenced what the students were willing to share. In addition, I wish we had had much more time—months—to talk with these students about their experiences. The conversations we had with students at both Northern and Southern College yielded such rich data. Over the years, I have tried to conduct follow-up interviews as the students graduated and moved on with their lives. I have remained in contact with several of the participants in various ways and have been thrilled to see their personal and professional successes continue. I remain eternally grateful to these exceptional individuals, who were so gracious in spending their time and sharing their insights with us. If you're reading this: I hope that I have done your stories justice and that you are as proud of your accomplishments as I am.

APPENDIX B

Student Profiles

NORTHERN COLLEGE STUDENTS

Adriana, 19, Female, Latina, Private/Urban

- Adriana was a first-year student but had attended a Catholic high school in a large Midwestern city, where she took mostly "advanced honors and AP" courses. She identified her religion as "Catholic" and left our question about social class blank. Adriana identified as an independent student. Her mother passed away when she was younger and she had no siblings. After her mother's death, Adriana lived with a family member.

Alexa, 19, Female, African American/Dominican, Public/Urban

- Alexa was a first-year student. She had attended a relatively small public high school in a large Midwestern city (her school was an experiment in the small schools movement). She reported taking mostly honors and some AP classes. She identified as agnostic and reported her social class as "lower class (maybe middle) not certain." Alexa was in the middle of her family, with four younger and four older siblings. On a demographic information sheet that we asked each student to fill out before their individual interview, Alexa drew a chart that represented her family and indicated whether her siblings had taken similar rigorous course loads as she had (it was a mix).

Araceli, 19, Female, Mexican American, Public/Urban

- Araceli was a first-year student when we interviewed her. She had attended a traditional public high school in a large southern city, where she enrolled in mostly "AP and honors" courses—the school began offering an international baccalaureate (IB) program after she had graduated. Her family had moved from the West Coast when she was in middle school. She identified as Roman Catholic and listed her social class as, "middle I think." Araceli was the middle of three children, but neither of her siblings took high-track courses.

Carla, 17, Female, African American, Public/Urban

- Carla was a first-year student when we interviewed her. She was by far our youngest participant, having just turned seventeen years old a few weeks before. She started at Northern College at just sixteen, having skipped two grades earlier in her K–12 career. She had attended a public high school in Illinois that specialized in STEM education. She identified as "Christian" and "lower class/low income." Carla grew up as the middle of three siblings. In response to our question about whether they also were in higher-track classes, she wrote, "older brother is in college. Little brother looks up to me."

Elsie, 19, Female, African American (Eritrean American), Public/Urban

- Elsie was also a first-year student when she participated in our project. She took "AP and honors" classes at a large traditional high school in Texas, which is where her parents immigrated to after leaving their home country of Eritrea. In her neat penmanship, she identified her religion as Roman Catholic and social class as "middle class." She had a sibling who was also enrolled in primarily advanced classes.

Emma, 18, Female, Puerto Rican, Public/Urban

- Emma was a first-year student when we interviewed her and reported taking "honors and AP" courses at her public high school in the large midwestern city where she grew up. The school offered an IB program, but she described it as very much a neighborhood school (as opposed to many of the students we interviewed, who had attended schools outside of their immediate neighborhood). She identified as "Christian" and "middle class" on her form. Emma was the oldest of four; she stated that two of her siblings were also taking higher-track courses.

Ice, 20, Male, African American, Public/Urban

- Ice was a second-year student when we met him. He was born in Chicago but had gone to high school less than an hour away from Northern College. He described his religion as "christian" and his social class as "working class." He came from a family of six siblings, two older and three younger, and described most as also high achieving. When asked to choose a pseudonym for the project, Ice was inspired by a particular brand of bottled water we had brought for the snack table.

Lillie, 20, Female, Latina/Mexican, Private/Urban

- Lillie was a second-year student when we interviewed her. She had attended an independent Catholic high school in her hometown, where she took a mix of "AP and honors" classes. She identified as "Catholic" and "middle class." Lillie was the youngest of three children but reported that she was the only one who took advanced classes.

Rick, 18, Male, Biracial (Puerto Rican and Black), Male/Private/Urban

- Rick was a first-year student when we first met him. Rick had attended an urban Jesuit college preparatory high school, where he took as many advanced classes as was allowed under school policy. It was important to him that we understand his identity as biracial: his father was Black and his mother was Puerto Rican, and he grew up in what he described as a "Puerto Rican household." He reported being "raised Roman Catholic" but was "more Christian" at the time we interviewed him. He reported his social class as "lower income." Rick had one older sister who he reported was taking "the same amount of AP classes" as he had.

Zion, 20, Male, African American, Male/Urban/Private and Urban/Public

- Zion was a second-year student when we interviewed him. He grew up in Louisiana and spent most of his high school years at a private high school there. However, he had spent his junior year in another state as a result of Hurricane Katrina. He described his religion as "christian" and his social class as "low middle class." Zion was the youngest of four children and described all but one as also high achieving.

Southern College Students

Carmen, 19, Female, Hispanic, Public/Urban

- Carmen was a second-year student when we met her. She had attended a traditional public high school in Texas, where she took AP courses. She identified as Roman Catholic and low-income. She had three older and one younger sibling; none of whom were in the same high track as she was.

Gregg, 19, Male, African American, Public/Suburban

- Gregg was a second-year student when we met him. He had gone to high school in a large public STEM magnet school in Texas and enrolled in IB courses. Gregg identified as "Christian" and "lower middle" in terms of his social class. He was the oldest of three siblings. When asked about them, he wrote, "sister into cosmetology, and brother wants to be an engineer."

Jessica, 20, Female, African American, Private/Suburban

- Jessica was a second-year student when we interviewed her. She had attended a traditional public high school in Louisiana, where she took "honors and AP courses." She identified as Baptist and working class. She had one older sibling who did not take the same classes that she did.

Melody, 19, Female, African American, Private/Urban

- Melody was a first-year student when we met her. She had attended private schools most of her life, including a Baptist high school where she was enrolled in mostly "AP and Honors courses." She identified as "Christian" and "middle class." She was the middle of three siblings and the only girl: she indicated that her brothers were "somewhat" enrolled in advanced classes similar to the ones she took.

Micayla, 18, Female, African American, Public/Urban

- Micayla was a first-year student when we met her. She had attended a traditional public high school that was ranked as one of the top public schools in her home state of Texas. She was enrolled in the IB program. She identified as Christian and middle class. She was the oldest of two siblings; she described her sister as "somewhat" on the same track as she was.

Moe, 19, Male, African American, Coed/Urban/Private

- Moe was a first-year student when we first met him. He grew up in Texas and had attended a private college preparatory boarding school. Moe came from a large family of six children. When we asked whether they were all high-achieving like him, he wrote, "Very much so." His father had passed away when he was younger, and he was raised by his mother, a nurse. Reflecting on his mother, he wrote, "I love her. I love my dad, too, my mom's just cuter. Living, yes, but also much cuter." He described his religious views as "christian" and his social class as "upper-lower class/lower-middle class."

Rita, 20, Female, Black, Public Magnet/Suburban

- Rita was a first-year student when we met her. She had attended a well-respected magnet school in her home state of Tennessee. She reported taking "all honors and AP courses (school is magnet and only offers these courses)." She identified as non-denominational Christian and her social class was "poor?" Rita was the middle of three siblings; she had an older brother who was in the military and a sister who went to cosmetology school.

Syril, 20, Male, Mexican, Public/Urban

- Syril was a third-year student when we met him. He had gone to a magnet high school in Texas, where he took gifted and talented as well as honors and AP courses. He reported his religion as "mixed—primarily Catholic now," and his social class as middle class. Syril was the middle of four children (two older and one younger); none of them took high-track classes.

Notes

PREFACE

1. Vanessa Siddle Walker, *Their Highest Potential: An African American School Community in the Segregated South* (Chapel Hill: The University of North Carolina Press, 1996).
2. Isabel Wilkerson, *The Warmth of Other Suns: The Epic Story of America's Great Migration* (London: Penguin Books); *Lovecraft Country*. (2020). Misha Green, creator. HBO. Based on the novel by Matt Ruff, *Lovecraft Country* (New York: HarperCollins Publishers 2016).
3. Walker, *Their Highest Potential*; James D. Anderson, *The Education of Blacks in the South, 1860–1935* (Chapel Hill: The University of North Carolina Press, 1988).
4. One useful history of this racist and ableist tradition particularly for Black children can be found in David J. Connor and Beth A. Ferri, "Integration and inclusion—A Troubling Nexus: Race, Disability, and Special Education," *The Journal of African American History* 90, no. 1–2 (2005): 107–127; Bettina L. Love, *We Want to Do More Than Survive: Abolitionist Teaching and the Pursuit of Educational Freedom* (New York: Beacon Press, 2019).
5. William Edward Burghardt Du Bois, *The Souls of Black Folk* (New Haven: Yale University Press, 2015).

INTRODUCTION

1. Some of these publications include Leslie Ann Locke, Lolita A. Tabron, and Terah T. Venzant Chambers, "If You Show Who You Are, Then They Are Going to Try to Fix You": The Capitals and Costs of Schooling for High-Achieving Latina Students," *Educational Studies* 53 (2017): 13–36; Lolita A. Tabron and Terah T. Venzant Chambers, "What Is Being Black and High Achieving Going to Cost Me in Your School? Students Speak Out About Their Educational Experiences Through a Racial Opportunity Cost Lens," *The High School Journal* 102, no. 2 (2019): 118–138; Terah T. Venzant

Chambers, "ROC'ing *Brown*: Understanding the Costs of Desegregation Using a Racial Opportunity Cost Framework," *Peabody Journal of Education* 94 (2019): 535–544; Terah T. Venzant Chambers, "Mergers and Weavers: Using Racial Opportunity Cost to Frame High-Achieving African American and Latino Students' School Culture Navigation Styles," *EAF Journal* 22, no. 2 (2011): 3; Terah T. Venzant Chambers and Kristin Shawn Huggins, "The Influence of School Factors on Racial Opportunity Cost for High-Achieving Students of Color," *Journal of School Leadership* 24, no. 1 (2014): 189–225; Terah T. Venzant Chambers, Kristin S. Huggins, Leslie A. Locke, and Rhonda M. Fowler, "Between a 'ROC' and a School Place: The Role of Racial Opportunity Cost in the Educational Experiences of Academically Successful Students of Color," *Educational Studies* 50, no. 5 (2014): 464–497; Terah T. Venzant Chambers, Leslie A. Locke, and Annel M. Tagarao, "'That *Fuego*, That Fire in Their Stomach': Academically Successful Latinas/os and Racial Opportunity Cost," *International Journal of Qualitative Studies in Education* 28, no. 7 (2015): 800–818.

2. Terah T. Venzant Chambers, "The 'Receivement Gap': School Tracking Policies and the Fallacy of the 'Achievement Gap,'" *The Journal of Negro Education* (2009): 417–431.
3. Du Bois, *The Souls of Black Folk.*
4. Angela Valenzuela, *Subtractive Schooling: U.S.-Mexican Youth and the Politics of Caring* (Albany: State University of New York Press, 1999).
5. See for example, David B. Tyack and Meryl Streep, *School: The Story of American Public Education* (Boston: Beacon Press, 2001).
6. See for example, David B. Tyack and Meryl Streep, *School: The Story of American Public Education* (Boston: Beacon Press, 2001).
7. See for example, David B. Tyack and Meryl Streep, *School: The Story of American Public Education* (Boston: Beacon Press, 2001).
8. See for example, David B. Tyack and Meryl Streep, *School: The Story of American Public Education* (Boston: Beacon Press, 2001). Also, Jeannie Oakes, *Keeping Track: How Schools Structure Inequality* (New Haven: Yale University Press, 2005).
9. See for example, David B. Tyack and Meryl Streep, *School: The Story of American Public Education* (Boston: Beacon Press, 2001). Also, Jeannie Oakes, *Keeping Track: How Schools Structure Inequality* (New Haven: Yale University Press, 2005).
10. See for example, Henry A. Giroux and Anthony N. Penna, "Social Education in the Classroom: The Dynamics of the Hidden Curriculum," *Theory & Research in Social Education* 7, no. 1 (1979): 21–42.
11. For one discussion of this history, see Richard Delgado and Jean Stefancic, *Critical Race Theory: An Introduction*. Vol. 20 (New York: NYU Press, 2017).

12. Joe R. Feagin, *The White Racial Frame: Centuries of Racial Framing and Counter-Framing.* (New York: Routledge, 2020).
13. Wendy Leo Moore, *Reproducing Racism: White Space, Elite Law Schools, and Racial Inequality* (New York: Rowman & Littlefield, 2007).
14. Eduardo Bonilla-Silva, *Racism Without Racists: Color-Blind Racism and the Persistence of Racial Inequality in the United States* (New York: Rowman & Littlefield, 2006).
15. Tukufu Zuberi and Eduardo Bonilla-Silva, eds., *White Logic, White Methods: Racism and Methodology* (New York: Rowman & Littlefield, 2008), 17.
16. Heidi Barajas and Amy Ronnkvist, "Racialized Space: Framing Latino and Latina Experience in Public Schools," *Teachers College Record* 109, no. 6 (2007): 1517–1538.
17. Lisa Delpit, "The Silenced Dialogue: Power and Pedagogy in Educating Other People's Children," *Harvard Educational Review* 58, no. 3 (1988): 280–299.
18. Beth Hatt, "Smartness as a Cultural Practice in Schools," *American Educational Research Journal* 49, no. 3 (2012): 438–460.
19. The notion of "ability" and even the idea of "objective" ability is obviously a contested area. Thus, the argument here is not to move from subjective to objective measures. Rather, we must acknowledge and challenge the racialized system that undergirds the process entirely and work to create school spaces that are more just. The ROC framework provides one roadmap to work toward that goal for Black and Latinx students. For further reading in this area see Robert J. Sternberg, "Who Are the Bright Children? The Cultural Context of Being and Acting Intelligent," *Educational Researcher* 36, no. 3 (2007): 148–155.
20. Terah T. Venzant Chambers and Lance T. McCready, "'Making Space' for Ourselves: African American Student Responses to Their Marginalization," *Urban Education* 46, no. 6 (2011): 1352–1378.
21. See for example, Herbert Kohl, *I Won't Learn From You: And Other Thoughts on Creative Maladjustment* (New York: The New Press, 1995).
22. Prudence L. Carter, *Keepin' It Real: School Success Beyond Black and White* (London: Oxford University Press, 2005), 307.
23. Venzant Chambers, "Mergers and Weavers."
24. Carter, *Keepin' It Real.*
25. Some recent examples include Chandra Arthur, "The Cost of Code Switching, TEDxOrlando, https://www.youtube.com/watch?v=Bo3hRq2RnNI; Kathleen Davis, "The Toll of Code-Switching and the Tyranny of Culture Fit," *Fast Company,* February 22, 2021, https://www.fastcompany.com/90605031/the-toll-of-codeswitching-and-the-tyranny-of-culture-

fit?fbclid=IwAR1UonuQ3_bg356eBnP7bAc5E2AZ0yuEXKLUcV4jfC3Kcj-xMCjaPwQ7I3U; Autumn Johnson, "Why I Left a White College for an HBCU," *Baltimore Sun*, December 26, 2019, https://www.baltimoresun.com/opinion/op-ed/bs-ed-op-1227-hbcu-20191226-myfo2oy6srczpeo6lj42pztjke-story.html?fbclid=IwAR3VWUpZhkZeJAF1cwA81Bqym-3Z-ogiCbt-F2LGF-wNXJe-iFRBXD0zpo0; Heather Jones, "Being Weird and Black Doesn't Mean You're Interested in Being White," *Wear Your Voice*, May 18, 2016, https://www.wearyourvoicemag.com/weird-black-doesnt-mean-youre-interested-white/?fbclid=IwAR3pg0jBz3hzo9-Ep_x8W82EN8cH2V6LsIcxF6NivPUB4-tfgkPF5wLTdqg; Natalie Morris, "People of Colour Have to 'Code-Switch' to Fit in With white Norms," *Metro*, March 3, 2020, https://metro.co.uk/2020/03/03/what-is-code-switching-12221478/?fbclid=IwAR2gnlHrf2Dw4vitMhmqQqrz7Tl_jtmXxgspC5M2ikPfxg7e7-VIhz64_sI.

26. Dorinda J. Carter Andrews, "The Construction of Black High-Achiever Identities in a Predominantly White High School," *Anthropology & Education Quarterly* 40, no. 3 (2009): 297.
27. Margaret A Gibson, *Accommodation Without Assimilation: Sikh Immigrants in an American High School* (Ithaca, NY: Cornell University Press, 1988).
28. Heidi L. Barajas and Jennifer L. Pierce, "The Significance of Race and Gender in School Success Among Latinas and Latinos in College," *Gender & Society* 15, no. 6 (2001): 873; Signithia Fordham, "Racelessness as a Factor in Black Students' School Success: Pragmatic Strategy or Pyrrhic Victory?," *Harvard Educational Review* 58, no. 1 (1988): 54–85.
29. Heidi L. Barajas and Jennifer L. Pierce, "The Significance of Race and Gender in School Success Among Latinas and Latinos in College," *Gender & Society* 15, no. 6 (2001): 873; Signithia Fordham, "Racelessness as a Factor in Black Students' School Success: Pragmatic Strategy or Pyrrhic Victory?," *Harvard Educational Review* 58, no. 1 (1988): 54–5.
30. Valenzuela, *Subtractive Schooling*.
31. Cornel West, *Race Matters* (New York: Routledge, 2018).
32. Delgado and Stefancic, *Critical Race Theory*.
33. Kimberlé W. Crenshaw, *On Intersectionality: Essential Writings* (New York: The New Press, 2017); Kimberlé W. Crenshaw, "Mapping the Margins: Intersectionality, Identity Politics, and Violence Against Women of Color," *Stanford Law Review* 43 (1990).
34. Venzant Chambers and McCready, "'Making Space' for Ourselves."
35. Barajas and Pierce, "The Significance of Race and Gender."

36. Sung Tae Jang, "The Schooling Experiences and Aspirations of Students Belonging to Intersecting Marginalisations Based on Race or Ethnicity, Sexuality, and Socioeconomic Status," *Race Ethnicity and Education* (2020): 1–22; See also Leah Schmalzbauer and Aleli Andres, "Stratified Lives: Family, Illegality, and the Rise of a New Educational Elite," *Harvard Educational Review* (2019): 635–660.
37. James S. Coleman, Ernest Campbell, Carol J. Hobson, James McPartland, Alexander Mood, Frederick D. Weinfield, and Robert L. York, *Equality of Educational Opportunity* (Washington, DC: U.S. Government Printing Office, 1966).
38. Borman and Dowling used sophisticated statistical modeling *using the original data* from the Coleman Report to show that schools mattered much more than was originally noted and also that in some cases even within-school differences could be attributed to teacher bias. Geoffrey Borman and Maritza Dowling, "Schools and Inequality: A Multilevel Analysis of Coleman's Equality of Educational Opportunity Data," *Teachers College Record* 112, no. 5 (2010): 1201–1246.
39. Richard R. Valencia, *Dismantling Contemporary Deficit Thinking: Educational Thought and Practice* (New York: Routledge, 2010).
40. Richard R. Valencia, *Dismantling Contemporary Deficit Thinking: Educational Thought and Practice* (New York: Routledge, 2010).
41. Debby Irving, *Waking Up White: And Finding Myself in the Story of Race* (Cambridge, MA: Elephant Room Press, 2016), xii.
42. Students selected their own pseudonyms; students' self-reported racial/ethnic identity was written on a student information sheet that we asked each student to complete prior to their individual interview.
43. In recent years, a number of publishers have announced their move to capitalize Black but not white. The *New York Times* offers a particularly useful discussion of the evolution of their decision: Deborah Coleman, "Why We're Capitalizing Black," *The New York Times,* July 5, 2020, https://www.nytimes.com/2020/07/05/insider/capitalized-black.html.
44. For one take on the controversy surrounding the term *Latinx* see Luis Noe-Bustamante, Lauren Mora, and Mark Hugo Lopez, "About One-in-Four U.S. Hispanics Have Heard of Latinx, but Just 3% Use It," August 11, 2020, *Pew Research Center,* https://www.pewresearch.org/hispanic/2020/08/11/about-one-in-four-u-s-hispanics-have-heard-of-latinx-but-just-3-use-it/.

CHAPTER 1

1. Some of the data that appear in this chapter were also used in Venzant Chambers and Huggins, "School Factors."
2. A copy of the letter sent by the school principal can be seen here: https://docs.google.com/viewerng/viewer?url=https://www.houstonisd.org//cms/lib2/TX01001591/Centricity/Domain/22431/Dress+Code.pdf
3. I have categorized school factors in this book a bit differently than in previous work. What is presented here represents my most updated thinking.
4. For a relatively recent review of literature in this area, see Christopher D. Slaten, Jonathan K. Ferguson, Kelly-Ann Allen, Dianne-Vella Brodrick, and Lea Waters, "School Belonging: A Review of the History, Current Trends, and Future Directions," *The Educational and Developmental Psychologist* 33, no. 1 (2016): 1–15.
5. Lisa Delpit, "The Silenced Dialogue: Power and Pedagogy in Educating Other People's Children," *Harvard Educational Review* 58, no. 3 (1988), 292.

CHAPTER 2

1. Some of the data that appears in this chapter were also used in Venzant Chambers, Huggins, Locke, and Fowler, "Between a 'ROC" and a School Place."
2. Danielle Sanders, "Black Students at the University of Chicago Lab High School Pen an Open Letter to School to Address Diversity and Racism on Campus," *Chicago Defender,* January 18, 2020, https://chicagodefender.com/black-students-at-the-university-of-chicago-lab-high-school-pen-an-open-letter-to-school-to-address-diversity-and-racism-on-campus/.
3. Microaggressions are "small, subtle, sometimes-unintended acts of discrimination." For the source of that definition as well as information on how to talk with young chidren about them, see Bret Turner, "Teaching First-Graders About Microaggressions: The Small Moments Add Up," *Learning for Justice,* March 26, 2019, https://www.learningforjustice.org/magazine/teaching-firstgraders-about-microaggressions-the-small-moments-add-up.
4. See for example Venzant Chambers, Huggins, Locke, and Fowler, "Between a 'ROC" and a School Place."
5. Keisha L. Bentley-Edwards, "Hope, Agency, or Disconnect: Scale Construction for Measures of Black Racial Cohesion and Dissonance," *Journal of Black Psychology* 42, no. 1 (2016): 73-99.
6. Signithia Fordham and John U. Ogbu, "Black Students' School Success: Coping With the 'Burden of 'Acting white''." *The Urban Review* 18, no. 3 (1986): 176-206.

7. Signithia Fordham and John U. Ogbu, "Black Students' School Success: Coping With the 'Burden of 'Acting white''." *The Urban Review* 18, no. 3 (1986): 176-206.
8. There is a growing amount of scholarship that addresses the negative implications of desegregation. While the racially segregated schools of the Jim Crow South were denied important material resources, there was a culture of care and community that the Black teachers in those schools cultivated. This is not an argument to return to segregated schools necessarily, but to point out that these schools offered tremendous value. For those interested in reading more about the positives that came out of schools in this era I strongly recommend Vanessa Siddle Walker's book, *Their Highest Potential,* as a place to start: Siddle Walker, *Their Highest Potential.*

CHAPTER 3

1. Some of the data in this chapter also appeared in Venzant Chambers, Locke, and Tagarao, "That *Fuego*, That Fire."
2. Cristian Benavides, "Students Walk Out After Teacher Orders: Speak 'American,'" *NBC News*, October, 16, 2017, https://www.nbcnews.com/news/latino/students-walk-out-after-teacher-tells-students-speak-american-n811256.
3. Zuberi and Bonilla-Silva, eds., *White Logic, White Methods.*
4. Aurora Chang, "Un-American: Latina High School Students' Testimonios of American and White Conflation in the Middle of Nowhere," *Race Ethnicity and Education* 20, no. 2 (2017): 240–251.

CHAPTER 4

1. Paul Tough, "How Kids Learn Resilience," *The Atlantic,* June 2016, https://www.theatlantic.com/magazine/archive/2016/06/how-kids-really-succeed/480744/.
2. Two examples include Sarah Ransdell, "Predicting College Success: The Importance of Ability and Non-Cognitive Variables," *International Journal of Educational Research* 35, no. 4 (2001): 357–364; Matthew R. Wawrzynski and Jody E. Jessup-Anger, "From Expectations to Experiences: Using a Structural Typology to Understand First-Year Student Outcomes in Academically Based Living-Learning Communities," *Journal of College Student Development* 51, no. 2 (2010): 201–217.
3. Angela Duckworth, "Grit: the Power of Passion and Perseverance," May 9, 2013, *TED*, https://www.youtube.com/watch?v=H14bBuluwB8&t=368s.

CHAPTER 4B

1. James D. Anderson, *The Education of Blacks in the South, 1860–1935* (Chapel Hill: The University of North Carolina Press, 1988).
2. Vanessa Siddle Walker, *Hello Professor: A Black Principal and Professional Leadership in the Segregated South* (Chapel Hill: The University of North Carolina Press, 2009); Vanessa Siddle Walker, *Their Highest Potential: An African American School Community in the Segregated South* (Chapel Hill: The University of North Carolina Press, 1996).

CONCLUSION

1. Youki Terada, "Why Black Teachers Walk Away," *Edutopia,* March 26, 2021, https://www.edutopia.org/article/why-black-teachers-walk-away.
2. Fordham and Ogbu, "Black Students' School Success."
3. For obvious reasons I cannot include the direct link to the report from Emma's school. However, for information about how *U.S. News* calculates their rankings, including the "College Readiness Index," see Robert Morse and Eric Brooks, "How *U.S. News* Calculated the 2021 Best High Schools Rankings," *U.S. News & World Report,* April 26, 2021, https://www.usnews.com/education/best-high-schools/articles/how-us-news-calculated-the-rankings.
4. See for example, Sean Kelly and Heather Price, "The Correlates of Tracking Policy: Opportunity Hoarding, Status Competition, or a Technical-Functional Explanation?," *American Educational Research Journal* 48, no. 3 (2011): 560–585.
5. Lolita Tabron, Courtney Mauldin, and I have collaborated to talk about this as "pay now or pay later." Tabron discusses this more fully in her ROC Talk that follows chapter 1.
6. See for example Venzant Chambers, "The 'Receivement Gap.'"
7. For two particularly compelling examples, see Terrance L. Green, "Community-Based Equity Audits: A Practical Approach for Educational Leaders to Support Equitable Community-School Improvements," *Educational Administration Quarterly* 53, no. 1 (2017): 3–39 and Tara J. Yosso, "Whose Culture Has Capital? A Critical Race Theory Discussion of Community Cultural Wealth," in *Critical Race Theory in Education* (New York, Routledge, 2014), 181–204.
8. Darrius A. Stanley and Terah T. Venzant Chambers, "The Case of Teacher Tracking at Leon Middle School," *Journal of Cases in Educational Leadership* 21, no. 3 (2018): 75–87.
9. See for example, Deborah Olsen, Sue A. Maple, and Frances K. Stage, "Women and Minority Faculty Job Satisfaction: Professional Role Interests, Professional Satisfactions, and Institutional Fit," *The Journal of Higher Education* 66, no. 3 (1995): 267–293.

10. See for example, Molly Ott and Jesus Cisneros, "Understanding the Changing Faculty Workforce in Higher Education: A Comparison of Non-Tenure Track and Tenure Line Experiences," *Education Policy Analysis Archives* 23 (2015): 90.
11. See for example, Anna Parkman, "The Imposter Phenomenon in Higher Education: Incidence and Impact," *Journal of Higher Education Theory and Practice* 16, no. 1 (2016): 51.
12. Natasha N. Croom, "Promotion Beyond Tenure: Unpacking Racism and Sexism in the Experiences of Black Womyn Professors," *The Review of Higher Education* 40, no. 4 (2017): 557–583; Willie J. Edwards and Henry H. Ross, "What Are They Saying? Black Faculty at Predominantly White Institutions of Higher Education," *Journal of Human Behavior in the Social Environment* 28, no. 2 (2018): 142–161.

CONCLUSION B

1. María Luísa González, personal communication, January 15, 2016.
2. Leslie A. Locke, "Finding My Critical Voice for Social Justice and Passing It On: An Essay," *International Journal of Qualitative Studies in Education 30* no. 1 (2017a), 83–96; Leslie A. Locke, "What's In Your Wallet?" Not Much Green, But a Whole Lotta White, *Whiteness and Education* 2, 32–47.
3. Venzant Chambers, Huggins, Locke, and Fowler, "Between a 'ROC" and a School Place"; Terah T. Venzant Chambers, Leslie A. Locke, and Annel M. Tagarao, "'That *Fuego*, That Fire in Their Stomach": Academically Successful Latinas/os and Racial Opportunity Cost." *International Journal of Qualitative Studies in Education* 28, no. 7 (2015): 800–818; Venzant Chambers, Locke, and Tagarao, "That *Fuego*, That Fire."
4. Yosso, "Whose Culture Has Capital?"
5. James Joseph Scheurich, ed., *Anti-Racist Scholarship: An Advocacy* (Albany: SUNY Press, 2012).; James Joseph Scheurich and Michelle D. Young, "Coloring Epistemologies: Are Our Research Epistemologies Racially Biased?" *Educational Researcher* 26, no. 4 (1997): 4–16.
6. Venzant Chambers and Huggins, "School Factors"; Venzant Chambers, Huggins, Locke, and Fowler, "A 'ROC' and a School Place."
7. See for example, Hani Morgan, "The Lack of Minority Students in Gifted Education: Hiring More Exemplary Teachers of Color Can Alleviate the Problem," *The Clearing House: A Journal of Educational Strategies, Issues and Ideas* 92, no. 4–5 (2019): 156–162.

APPENDIX A

1. Locke, Tabron, and Venzant Chambers, "If You Show Who You Are"; Tabron and Venzant Chambers, "Being Black and High Achieving"; Venzant Chambers, "ROC'ing *Brown*"; Venzant Chambers, "Mergers and Weavers"; Venzant Chambers and Huggins, "School Factors"; Venzant Chambers, Huggins, Locke, and Fowler, "A 'ROC' and a School Place"; and Venzant Chambers, Locke, and Tagarao, "That *Fuego*, That Fire."
2. As noted earlier, I use the terms *Black*, *Latinx*, and *racially minoritized* fairly consistently through the text but acknowledge and appreciate that students have a wide range of preferences in terms of identity. Thus, when speaking about a specific student, I try to use their preferred racial identity. Their self-described identities are also included in the participant profiles in Appendix B. I use the term *Latinx* in deference to its broader gender neutrality, but acknowledge that the term may or may not be broadly reflective of the preferences of the U.S. Latinx community. Ultimately, no one term is universally representative, and so I offer here explanations for why I have settled on these particular selections and respect that others might have chosen differently.
3. Students selected their own pseudonyms; students' self-reported racial/ethnic identity was written on a student information sheet that we asked each student to complete.

Acknowledgments

WHEN GRADUATE STUDENTS ASK ME what distinguishes those who finish their degrees, they are often surprised at my answer: perseverance. Perseverance is what pushes you to continue *when*, not *if*, you encounter unexpected roadblocks. Well, I have had to take my own advice many times over the course of writing this book. I lost my father somewhat unexpectedly after his months-long hospital stay following a relatively routine surgery, and received the official go-ahead for this book just days later. Add to that a global pandemic, racial protests, and a new job as a university administrator—let's just say, there were many days when I questioned whether I would complete this project. As I reflect on it now, I have come to understand that the advice I had given to my doctoral students was incomplete. Perseverance, yes. But also the love and support of people whose unrelenting belief in you will light your path through the darkest times. I would like to take a moment now to thank just a few of the light-bringers who encouraged me in this journey.

First, I thank my husband, Glenn Chambers, who has been part of this journey from the very beginning. He was there to hear me work out the foundational ideas for racial opportunity cost when it was just a collection of bare hopes and faint impressions. I have also benefited from his professional wisdom on a number of occasions. As a historian himself and author of two books, he is always my first call when I need help. Glenn, I love you with a depth I had no idea was possible. Thank you for teaching me what marriage could be. Thank you also to my son, Langston Malcolm Toure Chambers, who ended up being my unexpected writing coach. His timely and persistent encouragements meant everything. "Mom, aren't you supposed to be working on your book?" "How many words did you write today?" It did not escape me that he realized that my working on my book meant he had the freedom to play outside a little longer or sneak in a few extra minutes of screen time. Still, seeing the pride on his little face in knowing that his mom was writing a book: that was the best encouragement I could ever have imagined. I love you, Langston. We cannot wait to see what you will do to make a difference in this world with your huge heart, strong sense of determination, and insatiable humor. Your laugh is the best sound in the world to me. The irony of studying high-achieving Black students over the course of my career and then having one myself is not lost on me. I am inspired—and challenged—to live my commitments every day through my son.

Of course, I thank others in my family. Thank you, Mom, for teaching me that learning should be fun. That was her first and only real rule. My dad and I became much closer when I became an adult and I will always remain grateful that he and Langston developed such a strong bond before he passed. My aunt Reba taught me that investing in family and good friends will always matter more than material wealth. People who compare me to her flatter me beyond measure. I also appreciate the love and support of my family in Racine, WI, and Olive Branch, MS.

I'm grateful also to the three graduate students-turned professors who took a chance on working on this project, probably not understanding on the front end exactly what I was trying to do but joining me on this journey, anyway. Rhonda Fowler, Kristin Huggins, Leslie Locke: thank you.

It is hard to convey how much this book means to me, how important it was that I "get it right" and do justice to the students whose stories ended up in it as well as to the many, many more whose stories are represented here in spirit. In this effort, I relied on a few people to closely read pieces of this writing along the way and give critical feedback: Glenn Chambers, Delia Fernandez-Jones, Yomaira Figueroa, Leslie Gonzales, Jenni Mueller, Lolita Tabron, Estrella Torres: thank you.

I am also grateful to the many people and groups who physically wrote with me over the past year, encouraging me to keep going despite the many challenges I encountered. Yomaira, Estrella, Alyssa, and Leslie all participated in weekend writing retreats, where we holed up in hotel rooms at the peak of the COVID-19 pandemic. The absurdity and beauty of those moments will, I know, become treasured memories of this experience. The Diversity Research Network (DRN) at Michigan State also deserves huge kudos. The progress of this book can literally be measured by my involvement in their programs: I conceptualized the book proposal at a DRN writing retreat and put the final touches on the manuscript at another DRN writing retreat. The number of years between those two points will, I hope, be a secret that my DRN *familia* will help me keep. DRN friends Deborah Johnson, Beronda Montgomery, and James Earl Davis deserve particular acknowledgement. I also benefitted from the writing group known as CB1: Glenn Bracey, David McIntosh, Wendy Moore, Jenni Mueller, Phia Salter—not only are you some of the smartest people I know, you're also the kindest. There is also a secret social media group that certainly helped "bind" my thoughts together—I appreciate the wisdom provided by the women in that group.

Attending graduate school at the University of Illinois was a turning point in my life that offered lessons far beyond the classroom. I am grateful for the Latinx and Black communities who embraced me when I first arrived on campus—primarily because Martha Zurita put me in her car and drove me to campus; she saw something special in me and wanted to make sure I would survive *and thrive* amid the cornfields. I sure did. Special thanks to Annel, Brenci, Chamara, and Ishwanzya, who put up with my special brand of Minnesota quirkiness. I also thank Hugo, Jerrell, Jori, Katie, Kydalla, Maurice, Pita, Rashid, Rod, Shywon, and Toni (and the whole Illinois crew). I would not be the scholar let alone the person I am without your love.

When I write about my childhood experiences, particularly what it was like being a Black girl in a very white world, I am sure it comes across as though I had a terrible childhood. This could not be further from the truth. I remain eternally grateful to the people who helped create a community of love for me at various times in my life. Karen Bass, Susan Kinney Olsen, and Lisa McMurray were some of the best friends I could have asked for. My mom's family also could not have loved me harder. I cherish my memories of the farm in Symco: riding on the tractor with grandpa, eating endless special treats made with love by grandma, much-needed alone time with Aunt Marilyn, special occasions spent at Aunt Margie's, and endless rounds of tickle monster with Aunt Kathy. Thanks also to the folx at Salem Lutheran Church, who provided so much love and needed stability—particularly Kathy, Lori, and Maggie.

The life of an academic can be isolating because university jobs take you all over the place. We've been blessed to create networks of friends we consider family at both institutions where we've worked. At Texas A&M that included Jamilia Blake, Gwen Webb Hasan, Felipe and Maribel Hinojosa, Chance and Mechael Lewis, Dave and Sarah Louis, Anthony Rolle, Amanda Talley, and James and Lolita Tabron. At Michigan State we are grateful to Mónica Byrne-Jiménez, Michael and Dorinda Carter Andrews, Pero Dagbovie, Muhammad Khalifa and Nimo Abdi, Chris Dunbar and Reitu Mabokela, Yomaira Figueroa and Tacuma Peters, Delia Fernandez-Jones and Jonathan Jones, Terry Flennaugh and Joy Hannibal, Leslie Gonzales and Ruben Flores, LaShawn Harris, Jada Phelps, Gerardo López, Don and Elizabeth Lyons, Dylan Miner and Estrella Torres, Chezare Warren, Sheneka Williams, Terrion Williamson, and Jeff Wray and Tama Hamilton-Wray. And all of your cute, little (and not so little anymore) kids.

My appreciation also goes to Rich Milner for the honor of having this book included in his Race and Education Series of books and for the mentoring he has provided to me in my career, as well as to those involved in the publication process at Harvard Education Press, particularly the blind reviewers and the authors of the other books in the series.

Finally, immense and heartfelt thanks to the eighteen students who participated in this study. You are the heroes of this story.

About the Author

Terah Venzant Chambers, PhD is a professor of K–12 Educational Administration and associate dean for diversity, equity, and inclusion in the College of Education at Michigan State University. Her research interests include post-*Brown* K–12 education policy and urban education leadership. Specifically, she is interested in the ways in which within-school segregative policies influence the academic achievement and school engagement of Black students as well as the price of school success for high-achieving racially minoritized students (the racial opportunity cost). Dr. Chambers is past president of the University Council for Educational Administration (UCEA). She has served as coeditor for *AERA Open* and associate editor for *Educational Administration Quarterly*, the *Journal of Teacher Education*, and the *International Journal of Qualitative Studies in Education*. She has published in many of the field's top journals and received three separate outstanding reviewer awards from leading journals. She has an expertise in qualitative research methodologies, particularly critical approaches to research methods and theory. Dr. Chambers previously served as a congressional fellow with the Congressional Black Caucus Foundation (CBCF), with placements in the Office of Rep. Diane E. Watson (retired) and the Office for Civil Rights in the U.S. Department of Education. Dr. Chambers also serves on the East Lansing, Michigan, school board and is an ardent supporter of authentic university–community partnerships.

Index